John Phillips is Professor of French Literature and Culture at London Metropolitan University. He is the author of a number of books on French literature, including *Forbidden Fictions: Pornography and Censorship in Twentieth-Century French Literature* and *Sade: The Libertine Novels*. He is currently co-editing *The Encyclopaedia of Erotic Literature* for Routledge.

HOW TO READ

HOW TO READ

SADE

JOHN PHILLIPS

W. W. Norton & Company
New York   London

First published in Great Britain by Granta Publications

Marquis de Sade: Letters from Prison, translated by Richard Seaver, published by The Harvill Press. Used by permission of The Random House Group Limited. *Marquis de Sade: Juliette*, translated by Austryn Wainhouse, published by Arrow Books. Used by permission of the Random House Group Limited. 'Note on the Novel', Yale French Studies, No. 35 (1965), reproduced by permission of Yale French Studies, translation copyright © Richard Seaver. *Letters from Prison* by Marquis de Sade, published by Arcade Publishing, New York. *Justine, Philosophy in the Bedroom and Other Writings of the Marquis de Sade*, translated by Richard Seaver and Austryn Wainhouse. Copyright © 1965 by Richard Seaver and Austryn Wainhouse. Used by permission of Grove/Atlantic, Inc. *Juliette* by the Marquis de Sade, translated by Austryn Wainhouse. Copyright © 1968 by Austryn Wainhouse. Used by permission of Grove/Atlantic, Inc.

For information about permission to reproduce selections from this book, write to Permissions, W. W. Norton & Company, Inc., 500 Fifth Avenue, New York, N.Y. 10110

Manufacturing by The Maple-Vail Book Manufacturing Group
Production manager: Amanda Morrison

Library of Congress Cataloging-in-Publication Data

Phillips, John, 1950–
How to read Sade / John Phillips.—1st american ed.
p. cm.—(How to read)
"First published in Great Britain by Granta Publications."
Includes bibliographical references and index.
ISBN 0-393-32822-8 (pbk.)
1. Sade, marquis de, 1740–1814—Criticism and interpretation. I. Title.
II. How to read (New York, N.Y.)
PQ2063.S3P45 2005
843'.6—dc22
2005019138

W. W. Norton & Company, Inc., 500 Fifth Avenue, New York, N.Y. 10110
www.wwnorton.com

W. W. Norton & Company Ltd.
Castle House, 75/76 Wells Street, London W1T 3QT

1 2 3 4 5 6 7 8 9 0

CONTENTS

SERIES EDITOR'S FOREWORD

How am I to read *How to Read*?

This series is based on a very simple, but novel, idea. Most beginners' guides to great thinkers and writers offer either potted biographies or condensed summaries of their major works, or perhaps even both. *How to Read*, by contrast, brings the reader face to face with the writing itself in the company of an expert guide. Its starting point is that in order to get close to what a writer is all about, you have to get close to the words they actually use and be shown how to read those words.

Every book in the series is in a way a masterclass in reading. Each author has selected ten or so short extracts from a writer's work and looks at them in detail as a way of revealing their central ideas and thereby opening doors onto a whole world of thought. Sometimes these extracts are arranged chronologically to give a sense of a thinker's development over time, sometimes not. The books are not merely compilations of a thinker's most famous passages, their 'greatest hits', but rather they offer a series of clues or keys that will enable readers to go on and make discoveries of their own. In addition to the texts and readings, each book provides a short biographical chronology and suggestions for further reading and so on. The books in the *How to Read* series don't claim to tell you all you need to know about Freud, Nietzsche and Darwin, or indeed Shakespeare and the Marquis de Sade, but they do offer the best starting point for further exploration.

Unlike the available second-hand versions of the minds that have shaped our intellectual, cultural, religious, political and scientific landscape, *How to Read* offers a refreshing set of first-hand encounters with those minds. Our hope is that these books will, by turns, instruct, intrigue, embolden, encourage and delight.

Simon Critchley
New School for Social Research, New York

INTRODUCTION

'Sadism' is a term in common currency in English, and most will be well acquainted with its meaning. The term '*sadisme*' was originally coined in French in 1836 and later adopted as a medical term by Krafft-Ebing, the first sexologist, in the late nineteenth century. However, far fewer will be aware of the term's provenance. If people have heard of the Marquis de Sade at the beginning of the twenty-first century, they are most likely to dismiss him as an insane pornographer who suffered from an obsession with cruel and violent sex, and few of these will have actually ever read his work. This book is intended to introduce the contemporary reader to the real Sade, a Sade who is best discovered in and through his own words. This is particularly true of an author whose work has been clouded from the outset by myths, mostly negative ones (Sade the vivisector, the woman-beater, the child rapist and murderer are some of the more lurid examples). Conversely, the French surrealists of the last century were responsible for positive stereotypes that were just as inaccurate and misleading, enshrining the 'divine Marquis' as the arch-transgressor and apostle of unlimited freedom.

Sade is a figure of far greater complexity than allowed by any of the simplistic labels that have been pinned on him over the last two centuries; the Sade I will present is a creature of uncertainties and contradictions, but ultimately a profound and radical thinker, and an author of considerable intellect and erudition. His writings cover an extraordinarily broad spectrum, from fiction and plays to essays and personal correspondence. Sade's rhetorical talents, coupled with his gift for lucidity and precision, are notable in all of these genres, but he is perhaps most widely praised by critics for his skills as a writer of short stories and novellas, such as the original version of *Justine* and other so-called moral tales. The anonymous, obscene publications, the two novel-length versions of *Justine* and its sequel, *The Story of Juliette*, however, are certainly not lacking in literary qualities or philosophical interest, while some of the polemical essays are considered models of classical rhetoric. And although the overwritten melodramas he composed for the theatre have not attracted much critical interest to date, and are unlikely ever to do so, the intrinsic theatricality of Sade's thought and expression also helped to shape some of his most original non-dramatic work.

Reception of Sade's Works

Suspected throughout the 1790s as being the author of the infamous and anonymous *Justine*, Sade had already acquired a mythical status during his own lifetime. The very first review of the book, which appeared in the *Journal Général de France* on 27 September 1792, condemned it as 'disgusting and tiring to read', advising mature men to finish it in order to see how far human imagination can go, then to throw it in the fire. At the same time, the author of the review recognized that it was the work of a 'rich and brilliant mind'. Other critics of the time, such as Restif de la Bretonne, himself an author of erotic novels, condemned the work as cruel and corrupting. There was no acknowledgement of the book's philosophical content.

No doubt because of the scandal surrounding *Justine*, sales were brisk throughout the decade. In the nineteenth century, Sade's works, which also included *The Story of Juliette*, were published only clandestinely, and were more talked about than read, although many of the century's leading novelists and poets, such as Baudelaire, Flaubert, Stendhal and the Goncourt brothers in France, Byron and Swinburne in England, and Edgar Allan Poe in America, expressed admiration for Sade's work and claimed to draw inspiration from it. The more morally minded, of course, continued to condemn it. For the nineteenth-century French historian Michelet, Sade was the 'professor emeritus of crime' and as such typified the corrupt *ancien régime*, while another critic talked about the 'sulphurous smell' surrounding the Marquis de Sade. This kind of rhetoric merely strengthened Sade's mythical reputation as a monster of cruelty, who was probably insane into the bargain (a notion that arose from Sade's detention at the Charenton asylum during the final decade of his life, despite the resident physician's insistence that he could in no sense be described as mad).

From the end of the nineteenth century onwards, Sade's name came to be associated with the newly identified perversion of sadism, and his work became a reference-point for medical and psychiatric studies well into the twentieth. Sade's novels could therefore be read by specialists for *scientific* purposes, but were considered far too dangerous for general consumption. Nevertheless, the twentieth century saw the gradual evolution of more serious approaches to Sade's work as literature. Championed in the century's early decades by the poet Guillaume Apollinaire and the surrealists, and later by structuralists and post-structuralists, Sade's novels have been available in paperback in France since the 1960s, as well as in specialist academic editions, including the prestigious Pléiade series, badge of admission to the canon of French literature. In the US and the UK, the relaxation of book censorship initiated at the beginning of the 1960s eventually led to the general availability of the entire Sade canon from the 1970s. So, nowadays, anyone can read Sade, but the important question remains – *how* should he be read?

This book includes extracts from *Justine*, *Juliette*, and the anonymously published obscene dramatic dialogue *Philosophy in the Boudoir*. There are also passing references to *The 120 Days of Sodom*, which many consider to be Sade's most outrageous work of debauchery and perversion. All of these works are known as the 'libertine' novels, partly to distinguish them from Sade's more conventional writings, and it is for these novels that Sade's name has acquired its demonic reputation over the last two centuries.

The word 'libertinage' had come to mean 'free thinker on religion' by the end of the sixteenth century, but during the next 100 years it gradually took on the secondary meaning of debauchery. By Sade's time, a libertine was a person leading a dissolute life. In reality, such persons were male aristocrats or *nouveaux riches* of sufficient means to fund their indulgences. Libertine writing and painting were virtually synonymous with our modern term 'pornography'. In that they are vehemently anti-religious and depict wealthy and almost exclusively male libertine characters in scenes of debauchery using obscene language, Sade's libertine novels conform to both definitions of the word, and very few such novels were ever published under the author's real name for fear of imprisonment or worse. Severe penalties, including the guillotine, awaited both those found guilty of writing libertine works and their publishers.

It is on first encountering these libertine novels that the reader may experience some difficulty. This difficulty will not be a linguistic one (although the existing English translations do exhibit some oddities of style due to the translators' attempts to convey a flavour of eighteenth-century French).

The reader will certainly be shocked by some of the sexual perversions represented, but it is the sadistic cruelty of certain scenes and the philosophical justifications for this cruelty that these works appear to offer that many may find hard to stomach. Rare indeed is the reader who can complete one of these novels without ever having felt a sense of moral outrage or physical revulsion. In addition to torture and murder, they depict acts of paedophilia, sadomasochism, fetishism and perversion that are highly problematic from an ethical and moral standpoint. Yet it is these aspects of Sade's work that distinguish him from other materialist atheists of his time, and that make Sade unique in the history of literature and philosophy in the modern era. Sade fearlessly explores the darker side of human nature from which most of us would prefer to avert our gaze: the objectification of human beings, the utter selfishness of lust, the tyranny of an ego unfettered by laws or lacking the humanizing influences of socialization. Sade's exposure of the sexual motive that frequently lies behind human corruption and crime, of the sexual sadism that drives so much violence in human history, is a valuable message that bears repeating today. His work also makes positive contributions to current debates in sexual and gender politics, challenging norms of age, gender and sexuality, presenting woman as sexually autonomous, and undermining binary distinctions between young and old, male and female, hetero- and homo-sexuality. Sade's exceptional readiness to address the less palatable manifestations of human desire has arguably helped to normalize certain extreme sexual practices well before the liberalization of sexual mores in the late twentieth century, promoting a guilt-free perception of sodomy, coprophilia, bondage and other minority practices.

The violence and obscenity of Sade's novels inevitably raise the vexed question of the 'pornographic effect'; that is, can a direct causal link be established between the representation in writing of sexual crimes and the commission of such crimes in reality? The question is a complex one, and is bedevilled by the lack of any conclusive scientific evidence either way, despite the vociferous claims of some anti-pornography campaigners. Nevertheless, the issue is one of considerable relevance to a modern, technology-based culture, in which the private consumption of video and internet material is hard to assess in terms of effects on consumers. Readers will wish to form their own conclusions on this issue, which Sade's text continually brings to the fore.

In addition to Sade's importance as a key reference-point in current debates on obscenity and sexual politics, his work offers itself to a number of more focused approaches which provide further justification for reading him. I shall now briefly outline three such reading strategies, which will be deployed at various times during the course of this book, and which readers may find it useful to adopt themselves when tackling the novels on their own. Sade's libertine works can be viewed (1) as symptoms of an interesting psycho-pathological case; (2) in their historical and philosophical context; and (3) in the playful perspective of a text that we must beware of taking too seriously.

1. The Freudian Sade

The dramatic events of Sade's life, which included long periods of imprisonment for sodomy and blasphemy, have plausibly informed many critical readings of his work, leading to a predominance not only of biographies, but also of biographical studies of the novels, of which Simone de Beauvoir's long essay 'Must We Burn Sade?' is probably the best known. And as in many biographical approaches to literature, Freudian theories have held sway.

Among the conjectures that the application of such theories has produced, there have been a number of plausible hypotheses, for example, the link between imprisonment and sublimation, according to which the repression of Sade's sex-drive in prison was channelled constructively into an explosion of creativity. Whether as a consequence of sublimation or not, the prisoner certainly produced an astonishing quantity of writing. By the time he was released in 1790 after thirteen years behind bars, Sade had composed no fewer than eight novels and volumes of short stories, sixteen historical novellas, two volumes of essays, an edition of diary notes and some twenty plays, and this list does not include *The 120 Days of Sodom*.[1] Although the other major libertine novels were published during the few years of freedom Sade enjoyed in the 1790s, they, too, have their roots in work done in the Bastille in the 1780s.

More controversially, perhaps, the mother-hatred that seems to be a recurrent theme of the fiction has been attributed to maternal neglect throughout Sade's childhood, while some have argued that the anal/phallic and 'sadistic' focus of Sadeian sexuality is linked to unconscious father-worship. In this perspective, Sade would constitute a reverse oedipal case, hating the mother and loving the father.

To read Sade through the prism of Freudian theory is to read him as an interesting case-study, shifting the focus from the inexplicable horror of content to the fascinating detection of meaning. The reader thus becomes an analyst on an objective scientific quest, perhaps learning a little about him/herself along the way.

2. Historical Context

From our own twenty-first-century perspective, what shocks most when we read Sade is his transgressive representation of a sexuality that may be violent, incestuous and perverse. But Sade's work is rooted in the literary, philosophical and political climate of eighteenth-century France, and makes little sense when read outside of this historical context. Indeed, the ahistorical Sade of some popular readings can only be a perverted and insane pornographer.

On a literary level, Sade must therefore be read as a libertine writer within an existing tradition, dating back to the mid-seventeenth century, a tradition from which he borrows extensively. Many well-known writers before Sade, including the philosophers Diderot and Mirabeau, had composed and published libertine works. Indeed, there was a lively commerce in illicit books in Paris throughout the eighteenth century, particularly in the years leading up to the Revolution. During this period, 'philosophical books', as they were known in the trade, included any work considered subversive by the authorities, from religious satires to political pamphlets attacking the monarchy. Obscenity was often used in such works as a satirical weapon to castigate a corrupt clergy and a decadent aristocracy. Driven partly by similarly satirical intentions, Sade's obscene writings cannot be properly read outside this literary historical context.

Certainly his representation of libertinage is more extreme, more graphic and more horrific than that of any of his predecessors or contemporaries. In our own predominantly

secular age, it is this depiction of a permissive, perverse and
violent sexuality that carries the most transgressive charge. In
contrast, an eighteenth-century society steeped in Catholicism
would have found the atheistic basis of his moral philosophy
and his blasphemous rejection of all religious belief far more
intolerable.

Sade's atheism was heavily influenced by the work of two
materialist philosophers of the Enlightenment: La Mettrie's
Man Machine (1748) and Baron d'Holbach's *System of Nature*
(1770). Materialism rejected belief in a soul or afterlife, reducing everything in the universe to the physical organization of
matter. According to La Mettrie, scientific observation and
experiment are the only means by which human beings can
be defined, and this method tells us that Man is quite simply
a machine, subject to the laws of motion like any mechanism
of eighteenth-century science. The sole purpose of existence
in this scheme of things is pleasure – a doctrine espoused
with relish by so many of Sade's libertine characters.
D'Holbach views the human being as a collection of atoms, so
that even the conscience has a material origin, acquired from
our education and experience. His system does not, therefore,
allow for free will, since all our decisions are determined by
our personal interest. For d'Holbach, all morality is a matter of
social utility or pragmatism.

Sade described *System of Nature* as the true basis of his philosophy, and, indeed, lifted whole passages from it practically
verbatim to place in the mouths of his protagonists, as they
railed against the various dogmas of religion. As atheistic
materialism's most powerful and most controversial voice,
Sade is the dark side of the Enlightenment because he says
loud and clear what other Enlightenment philosophers hardly
dare to whisper: the death of God and the renaissance of Man
from the ashes of a God-centred universe. He must therefore

be read against the background of this materialist tradition, which he extends and reinterprets in his own fashion.

In Sade's anonymous novels, *Philosophy in the Boudoir*, *The New Justine*, and *The Story of Juliette*, the circumlocution and euphemism of the two earlier versions of *Justine* give way to vulgarism and obscenity, as the abstractions of the libertine dissertation find concrete illustration in descriptions of the sexual acts that precede and follow it. In the many lengthy descriptions of these acts, Sade's language eschews the metaphorical, providing direct access to the body, its sexual parts and functions. Here, materialism translates itself into a transparent materiality of language. It is usual, of course, for the vocabulary of erotic literature to focus on the body. Sade's originality, however, lies in placing this body at the centre of his atheistic philosophy, in siting philosophy *in* the boudoir, in making sex the driving force of all human action more than a century before Freud.

3. Games Sade Plays

As you will discover in this book, there are many Sades, and it is not always easy to distinguish the man of letters from the hypocritical pornographer, the monarchist from the republican, the satirist from the polemicist. Nevertheless, it is the very mobility of Sade's thought and the sometimes elusive character of meaning in his writing that is intriguing and stimulating. If we are to sum him up in a single phrase, however, we might call him an arch-cynic, a questioning voice determined to unpick the threads of all self-righteous orthodoxies, to deflate pomposities and expose inconsistencies and hypocrisies. Indeed, the reader will discover that Sade's text frequently strikes a satirical, ironic or parodic note. Sade is the devil's advocate of philosophical debate, and the more extreme passages in his work are best read as exercises, designed to push the logic of atheistic materialism to its ultimate conclusion.

The satirical is a major aspect of Sade's playfulness. For example, he scathingly lampoons Rousseau's idealistic view of human nature on numerous occasions, and in the sexual perversion of the fifteen-year-old Eugénie in *Philosophy in the Boudoir* there is an implicit parody of Rousseau's educational philosophy, specifically, the notion that sexual knowledge should be kept from the young as long as possible.

At other times, Sade's narrator plays games with his reader, for example, alluding teasingly to secret activities of which even he has no knowledge. Such games can be frustrating, but also stimulating for a reader intent on tracking down meaning and resolving enigmas. Sade's textual games compel the reader to play a more active part in the creative process through conjecture and speculation.

At a philosophical level, this game strategy appears designed to make us question received wisdoms of faith, ethics and morality and rethink the entire nature of existence as a random material event, ultimately devoid of meaning.

The Marquis de Sade's work is vast in scope and has many extraordinary qualities. From a purely literary point of view, Sade certainly deserves a place as an author of considerable merit. In addition to the sheer breadth of his vision and the astonishing range of his work across many genres, Sade made a number of important contributions to an existing literary tradition, some of which we shall see later. But he will always be best remembered for his achievements as a pioneering explorer of human sexuality, which follow directly from his materialist thinking.

Sade's work deserves to be read because self-knowledge is

always preferable to ignorance or denial, authenticity to hypocrisy. And to read in search of truth, as Sade himself knew well, is the most moral of acts: 'I speak only to those who are capable of understanding me, and those people will read me without risk.' Rather than burn Sade, we must allow him to show us the potential for evil that exists within us all, the better to understand and confront it.

The chapters that follow are intended to provide representative samples of Sade's work in both fiction and non-fiction. Extracts have been chosen, not for their fame, but rather because they are of intellectual, literary, philosophical or political interest. After an excursion in Chapter 1 into the hazardous territory of authorial personality, Chapters 2 to 5 are respectively devoted to the exposition in Sade's texts of views on religion, sex, politics and the novel, while Chapters 6 to 8 focus on aspects of the fiction that have proved controversial in modern sexual and gender politics. Chapter 9 looks at a highly innovative characteristic of the writing – what we might call the dramatization of prose – that marks him out from other writers of his age. The question of Sade's legacy, already touched on in this introduction, is revisited in Chapter 10, which offers a more detailed assessment of the influence of his work since the eighteenth century.

Finally, this is a book about reading, and we hope that our reader will find it useful as a guide through the maze of Sade's vast and complex œuvre. The very least we can say is that the reader has continually remained at the forefront of our mind during the writing process, a plural reader with a variety of tastes and tolerances. In striving to please each taste and satisfy every tolerance, while at the same time acknowledging the impossibility of doing so, we are following the splendid example set by the narrator of Sade's first major libertine work.

However, we are certainly not aiming to please or satisfy in quite the same fashion . . .

Many of the extravagances you are about to see illustrated will doubtless displease you, yes, I am well aware of it, but there are amongst them a few which will warm you to the point of costing you some fuck, and that, reader, is all we ask of you; if we have not said everything, analysed everything, tax us not with partiality, for you cannot expect us to have guessed what suits you best. Rather, it is up to you to take what you please and leave the rest alone, another reader will do the same, and little by little, everyone will find himself satisfied.

Introduction, *The 120 Days of Sodom*

1

FACTS AND FICTIONS

Vincennes, February 1781

Yes, I am a libertine, that I admit. I have conceived everything that can be conceived in that area, but I have certainly not practised everything I have conceived and never shall. I am a libertine, but I am neither a *criminal* nor a *murderer*, and since I am obliged to place my apology next to my justification, I shall therefore say that 'tis quite possible that they who condemn me so unfairly are in no position to offset their infamies by good deeds as patent as those I can raise to compare to my misdeeds. I am a libertine, but three families living in your section of the city lived for five years on my charity, and I rescued them from the depths of poverty. I am a libertine, but I saved a deserter from the military, a man abandoned by his entire regiment and his colonel, from certain death. I am a libertine, but at Evry, with your entire family looking on, I saved at the risk of my own life a child who was about to be crushed beneath the wheels of a cart drawn by runaway horses by throwing myself beneath the cart. I am a libertine, but I have never compromised the health of my wife. I have never indulged in any of the other branches of libertinage so often fatal to the fortune of one's children [. . .] have I not always loved everything that was deserving of my love, and everything I ought to hold dear? did I not love my father? (alas, I still weep for him every day of my life) did I ever behave badly with my mother? and was it not when I went to be with her as she drew her last breath, and to show her the

> ultimate mark of my devotion, that your mother had me dragged off
> to this horrible prison, where she has left me to languish for the past
> four years? [. . .] If I am a murderer, I did not commit enough mur-
> ders, and if I am not, I shall have been punished far too severely and
> I have every right to demand redress.
>
> *Marquis de Sade: Letters from Prison*

The difficulty of distinguishing a single authorial voice from a multitude of other personas is a particular feature of Sade's work, even in the non-fictional texts such as his personal correspondence, where one might expect to be reading the author's unambiguous thoughts and views.

Sade's letters and journals are, on the face of it, autobiographical in nature, but they are texts like any other and must be read with caution. The temptation to fictionalize the self is ever-present in all forms of autobiography, and Sade the actor and dramatist was notoriously prone to play roles as much off the stage as on it. (Sade was active in the staging of plays from a young age, and indeed often assumed leading roles in his productions.) The two passages quoted in this chapter appear to represent two different and, in certain respects, conflicting authorial personas. The juxtaposition of these passages underlines the Marquis's role-playing tendencies and the ultimate impossibility of identifying the real Sade through his writing. The most one can achieve, perhaps, is the recognition of particular traits of character and temperament.

Letter-writing fulfilled a number of different functions for the incarcerated aristocrat: much-needed therapy, a positive activity to while away those long hours of confinement, a discourse with himself, and, of course, the main form of communication with the outside world. And as documentary evidence of the Marquis's changing states of mind during his time in prison, the letters are unique in the Sade canon of writings.

The first extract is from one of the many letters the Marquis sent to his wife, Renée-Pélagie, from prison. Sade endured two long periods of imprisonment: the first from 1777 until 1790, and the second from 1801 until 1814. He certainly committed a number of acts that some might now consider reprehensible, acts that included the flagellation and buggery of prostitutes and, allegedly, the sexual corruption of young women, although there is no reason to believe that any of this behaviour involved compulsion. Nevertheless, in 1772, the thirty-two-year-old Sade and his valet were condemned to death for crimes of sodomy (which was a capital offence in eighteenth-century France) and the attempted poisoning of young prostitutes in Marseilles. In fact, although he may well have been guilty of buggery, Sade had merely given the young women pastilles containing Spanish fly, a well-known aphrodisiac which also caused flatulence – an effect the Marquis found sexually arousing. Following a protracted cat-and-mouse game with the authorities, which included a flight to Italy with his sister-in-law and brief spells in captivity, Sade was eventually caught and imprisoned indefinitely under a *lettre de cachet*, or royal warrant, according to which individuals might be held in prison at the King's pleasure for indefinite periods without trial, and which his mother-in-law, the Présidente de Montreuil, employed to devastating effect in Sade's own case. (The Présidente owed her title and considerable influence at court to her husband's position as chief judge of one of Paris's highest courts of law.) She used her influence to ensure that her wayward and embarrassing son-in-law was kept under lock and key from the late 1770s until 1790, when the *lettre de cachet* was abolished following the Revolution, and all those detained under it were released. *Justine* and *Juliette* did not appear until the 1790s, while *The 120 Days of Sodom* was never in the public domain during his lifetime.

When Sade was eventually locked up for the books he wrote, he was over sixty years old. In 1801 he was arrested at his publisher's in Paris, allegedly with a copy of the newly printed *Juliette* in his hand.

During his first long spell of imprisonment in the Château de Vincennes and subsequently the Bastille, where he was transferred in 1784, Sade wrote a huge number of letters, mostly addressed to Renée-Pélagie, and even letters to others, such as his notary, had to pass through her hands. This extract from Sade's self-styled 'Grand Letter', written to his wife from the dungeon of Vincennes to mark the fourth anniversary of his imprisonment, represents one of a number of attempts on his part to distance himself from the kind of behaviour exhibited by his fictional libertines. 'I have conceived everything that can be conceived in that area' might describe his first and most horrific libertine novel, *The 120 Days of Sodom*, which offers the reader a menu of 600 'passions' or perversions. Sade's claim not to have practised everything he has conceived, however, is indeed supported by the known historical facts: there is no indication that the Marquis was ever seriously suspected of having committed any of the appalling crimes represented in his anonymous fictions.

When referring to those who condemned him 'so unfairly', Sade undoubtedly has in mind all the hypocritical and corrupt agents of the *ancien régime* who ruled the courts, while lining their own pockets and, like the magistrate who tries the unfortunate Justine, masturbating under their robes as they sentence unfortunates to the gallows. He would also be thinking of the grossly unjust system of the *lettre de cachet*.

The extract also demonstrates a growing paranoia that was to become a marked feature of Sade's correspondence in his later years at Charenton. A number of artful self-defensive strategies (charity, heroism, marital devotion) are put into effect here by a man who is familiar with all things theatrical. On the other hand, there is some evidence that the Marquis was not incapable of the generosity he claims for himself, even towards those who wronged him. During the early years of the Revolution, citizen Sade rose to the office of magistrate. When chance placed his in-laws' death-warrants before him, and he had a perfect opportunity to avenge himself for the thirteen years of imprisonment he had endured – for which Sade held his mother-in-law entirely responsible – he refused to sign them.

Above all, perhaps, Sade's 'Grand Letter' bears witness to an urgent and deep-seated need to be loved and understood which can perhaps be traced back to a childhood marred by parental absence and neglect. This need will surface repeatedly and in many different guises in the fictional works.

Related, on my mother's side, to the greatest men in the kingdom and, through my father, to the most distinguished families of the province of Languedoc; born in Paris in the bosom of luxury and abundance, I believed, just as soon as I was able to reason, that nature and fortune had combined to lavish their gifts upon me; I believed it because people were foolish enough to tell me so, and this ridiculous prejudice made me haughty, despotic, and choleric; it seemed that everything must yield to me, that the entire universe must flatter my whims, and that it was enough for me to conceive them for them to be satisfied. I shall relate just one feature of my childhood to convince you of the dangerous principles that were so ineptly allowed to take root in me. Since I was born and raised in the palace of the illustrious prince to whom my mother had the honour to be related, and who was about my age, I was encouraged to share his company so that, having befriended him in infancy, I might enjoy his support throughout life; but in the course of our youthful games, my vanity, which as yet knew nothing of such calculations, was offended by a quarrel over some object or other; and since he seemed to think he was entitled to it because of his superior rank (doubtless he had every right to think so), I avenged myself for his resistance with numerous blows, without a single thought for the consequences, such that only violent force was able to separate me from my adversary.

Aline et Valcour, my translation

This second extract is taken from the opening pages of Sade's long epistolary novel, *Aline et Valcour*, which he wrote during his long years of imprisonment in the Bastille in the 1780s and published under his own name in the 1790s.

Aline et Valcour was written when the author was in his forties, but the remarkable vividness of this scene underlines two things: the force and significance of the memory in question, and the relationship between Sade's life and work. Although, as we have already seen, the work and the life are not to be confused, certain experiences such as Sade's long period of imprisonment in the Bastille, the boredom and the sexual deprivations that this entailed may have been important stimuli for the fictional writing.

Born in 1740, Donatien Alphonse François de Sade spent his early years in the luxurious surroundings of the Condé palace in Paris. The Condé family were closely related to the ruling Bourbons, and the Prince de Condé, who was Sade's almost exact contemporary, was a prince of the royal blood. The little marquis was brought up alongside the little prince because Donatien's mother was related to the prince's father and served as a governess and lady-in-waiting to the prince.

In the novel's opening pages, the young hero Valcour describes a childhood quarrel with a child who closely resembles the young Prince de Condé, and the argument bears a striking similarity to a real event in the author's early life.

Many critics have noted the autobiographical similarities in Valcour's character in particular the description of despotic tendencies, an incipient stubbornness, an unbridled ego and an uncontrollable temper – the seeds of the disastrous temperament that would prove the adult Sade's undoing. At the time of this incident, Donatien was only three years old. The account here, penned many years later during his long stay in the Bastille, nevertheless displays a moving self-knowledge, and its position towards the beginning of the novel suggests the importance of the memory. Indeed, in many significant respects, this is a key passage for understanding the personality of the infant who was to become history's infamous Marquis. The passage also throws light on approaches to Sade's work, helping to explain in particular the seductiveness of biographical readings of Sade's fictional work, readings that, as we saw in the Introduction, are often rooted in Freudian psychoanalysis.

In any event, Valcour's portrait recalls aspects of Sade's own life. Like his hero, Sade comes from a distinguished aristocratic line in the Languedoc that dates back to the Middle Ages. Like Valcour, he was born in Paris 'in the bosom of luxury and abundance'. Such wealth and lineage helped to induce in the young Donatien a pride, bordering on arrogance, that would last throughout his life, and that finds repeated echoes in his writings. Both Valcour and Sade were favoured by nature, as well as fortune. The infant Sade had angelic good looks: fine features, blue eyes and curly blond hair. The only surviving contemporary portrait of the Marquis, by the artist Van Loo, depicts a rather effeminate-looking young man with pouting good looks and a stylish wig, and there is plenty of evidence in letters from those who knew him that Sade had a charismatic personality that attracted women like a magnet from his teens until well into his seventies. As with Valcour, moreover, people were certainly foolish enough to tell him how favoured he was. Although his own mother appeared to neglect him, he was cosseted and spoilt by a paternal grandmother and five aunts who showered gifts on the only boy in the family, indulging his every whim. The Marquis's seductive charm and sensitive character would soften the hearts of many other women in the years to come.

Valcour's portrait is in the nature of a self-confession, showing a readiness on the part of the middle-aged Marquis to acknowledge the flaws in his character that led to his downfall. The object of contention between the two boys was doubtless some insignificant toy, but its true significance was symbolic. For, like his authorial counterpart, the young Valcour not only thought himself superior in status to the royal prince, but he was also confident that his superior strength would make him the victor. Valcour's despotic assumption that 'the entire universe must flatter [his] whims' finds repeated echoes in Sade's libertine fictions. In *The Story of Juliette*, for instance, the wicked libertines Saint-Fond and Noirceuil frequently reduce all else to the satisfaction of their merest desires, justifying this megalomania in terms of a self-interest which they identify as the imperative governing all of nature, including humankind. Almost all of Sade's libertine protagonists reject religious belief as superstitious nonsense, and yet appear to want to take God's place, or at the very least to rival nature which they view as a quasi-divine force. This thirst for absolute power reminds us of Sade's own experience of the Revolution. The born-again republican was better placed than most to witness the bloody consequences of despotism as the guillotine blade repeatedly rose and fell before his eyes (see Chapter 4). Yet Sade's fictional libertine takes on a life of his own, escaping the author's control to become an iconic superhero for later thinkers. Nietzsche's superman and Bataille's 'sovereign man', for instance, seem directly inspired by the Sadeian model. Both Nietzsche and Bataille had read Sade's works and admired them greatly.

Valcour's contempt for the stupidity of those who indulged him ('people were foolish enough to tell me so') suggests a disdain for those of inferior rank and intelligence, a calculating self-interest which we can identify as life-long characteristics of the author himself. Valcour concedes that 'dangerous principles' were 'allowed to take root' in him, demonstrating Sade's lucid self-awareness. At the same time, however, Valcour simultaneously neutralizes this concession in a single word, 'ineptly': the fault, in other words, lay not with him but with those foolish enough to indulge him. Sade himself expresses similar sentiments in his correspondence from prison. Again, a scarcely concealed contempt for the weakness of others contained in this single word is mirrored in the doctrines of egoism and *isolisme* at the heart of Sade's philosophy, that is, the conviction that every human being is utterly alone. Christianity, for example, is scorned by Sade's libertines, partly because it defends the weak against the strong and so infringes a fundamental law of nature, according to which only the strong are allowed to survive. This self-interest is reflected in the somewhat barefaced admission by Valcour that his friendship with the 'illustrious prince' has the sole aim of securing his support throughout life, although this remark may also be read as an ironic comment on a pre-revolutionary society, ruled by an aristocratic élite determined at all costs to preserve their privileged status.

Valcour's violent response to the prince 'without a single thought for the consequences' is characteristic, too, of Sade's own behaviour, of his incurable tendency to take foolhardy risks, acting on impulse to satisfy the desires of the moment, putting his pleasure first and the interests of others, and at times even his own safety, last. We may conjecture that the publication of *The New Justine* and *The Story of Juliette*, his most obscene and most violent published works, in the late

1790s was an extremely hazardous venture under a repressive Napoleonic regime which employed police spies to root out subversive or pornographic writings.

The final observation here that 'only violent force was able to separate me from my adversary' suggests another recognizable author trait: a force of will that Sade displays throughout his life, driving an unshakable self-belief and a dogged determination.

The strongly autobiographical vein of this opening passage in one of the Marquis de Sade's major novels reveals a profound need on the author's part to put his case to the public, to suggest that the libertine ways of his twenties and thirties were the logical consequence of his childhood.

2

BETWEEN HEAVEN AND EARTH

Sade's first prose work, the delightful short 'parable' *Dialogue between a Priest and a Dying Man*, was composed in prison in 1782. The work consists of a conversation at the moment of death between a dying man and a Catholic priest come to administer the last rites and hear the man's last confession so that he might embrace the Lord and enter paradise. Sade's very choice of situation is a masterstroke, in that it provides the perfect opportunity to re-examine the logical basis of all religious belief. We join the debate towards the end of the *Dialogue*, after the moribund hero has efficiently dispatched the standard theological views put forward by the hapless cleric.

> PRIEST: But you must surely believe something awaits us after this life, you must at some time or another have sought to pierce the dark shadows enshrouding our mortal fate, and what other theory could have satisfied your anxious spirit, than that of the numberless woes that betide him who has lived wickedly, and an eternity of rewards for him whose life has been good?
>
> DYING MAN: What other, my friend? that of nothingness, it has never held terrors for me, in it I see naught but what is consoling and unpretentious; all the other theories are of pride's composition,

this one alone is of reason's. Moreover, 'tis neither dreadful nor absolute, this nothingness. Before my eyes have I not the example of Nature's perpetual generations and regenerations? Nothing perishes in the world, my friend, nothing is lost; man today, worm tomorrow, the day after tomorrow a fly; is it not to keep steadily on existing? And what entitles me to be rewarded for virtues which are in me through no fault of my own, or again punished for crimes wherefor the ultimate responsibility is not mine? how are you to put your alleged god's goodness into tune with this system, and can he have wished to create me in order to reap pleasure from punishing me, and that solely on account of a choice he does not leave me free to determine?

PRIEST: You are free.

DYING MAN: Yes, in terms of your prejudices; but reason puts them to rout, and the theory of human freedom was never devised except to fabricate that of grace, which was to acquire such importance for your reveries. What man on earth, seeing the scaffold a step beyond the crime, would commit it were he free not to commit it? We are the pawns of an irresistible force, and never for an instant is it within our power to do anything but make the best of our lot and forge ahead along the path that has been traced for us. There is not a single virtue which is not necessary to Nature and conversely not a single crime which she does not need and it is in the perfect balance she maintains between the one and the other that her immense science consists; but can we be guilty for adding our weight to this side or that when it is she who tosses us onto the scales? no more so than the hornet who thrusts his dart into your skin.

PRIEST: Then we should not shrink from the worst of all crimes.

DYING MAN: I say nothing of the kind. Let the evil deed be proscribed by law, let justice smite the criminal, that will be deterrent enough; but if by misfortune we do commit it even so, let's not cry over spilled milk; remorse is inefficacious, since it does not stay us from crime, futile since it does not repair it, therefore it is absurd to beat one's breast, more absurd still to dread being punished in another world if we have been lucky to escape it in this. God forbid that this be construed as encouragement to crime, no, we should avoid it as much as we can, but one must learn to shun it through reason and not through false fears which lead to naught and whose effects are so quickly overcome in any moderately steadfast soul. Reason, sir – yes, our reason alone should warn us that harm done our fellows can never bring happiness to us and our heart; that contributing to their felicity is the greatest joy Nature has accorded us on earth; the entirety of human morals is contained in this one phrase: Render others as happy as one desires oneself to be, and never inflict more pain upon them than one would like to receive at their hands. There you are, my friend, those are the only principles we should observe, and you need neither god nor religion to appreciate and subscribe to them, you need only have a good heart. But I feel my strength ebbing away; preacher, put away your prejudices, unbend, be a man, be human, without fear and without hope forget your gods and your religions too: they are none of them good for anything but to set man at odds with man, and the mere name of these horrors has caused greater loss of life on earth than all other wars and all other plagues combined. Renounce the idea of another world; there is none, but do not renounce the pleasure of being happy and of making for happiness in this. Nature offers you no other way of doubling your existence, of extending it. – My friend, lewd pleasures were ever dearer to me than anything else, I have idolized them all my life and my wish has been to end it in their bosom; my end draws near, six women lovelier than the light of day are waiting in the chamber adjoining, I have reserved them for this moment, partake of the feast with me, following my example embrace them instead of the vain sophistries of superstition, under their caresses strive for a little while to forget your hypocritical beliefs.

NOTE

The dying man rang, the women entered; and after he had been a little while in their arms the preacher became one whom Nature has corrupted, all because he had not succeeded in explaining what a corrupt nature is.

Dialogue between a Priest and a Dying Man

This extract deals with a central theme in Sade's work: the total rejection of all religious belief, including the notion of an afterlife. This dramatized philosophical essay also illustrates a number of other fundamental Sadeian concepts: the quasi-divine role of nature, a mechanistic view of life and yet, at the same time, the perpetual transmutability of all living matter, a relativistic and pragmatic approach to morality, and, given the brevity of human life, and youth in particular, the importance of taking every opportunity to indulge in physical pleasures.

This early work is in the dialogue form that was a traditional vehicle for seventeenth- and eighteenth-century pornography, as well as for philosophical essays, in all European languages (in sixteenth-century Italy, Aretino's *Ragionamenti* became the model for such works), and which Sade himself would favour in *Philosophy in the Boudoir*, the obscene work he would write more than a decade later. Although this dialogue is not explicitly obscene, it is certainly libertine in terms of its overall philosophical message and its preoccupation with the physical body and sexual pleasure, and, in that sense, it is a precursor of the sexually explicit writings that the Marquis would shortly compose (*The 120 Days of Sodom*, for instance, is dated by scholars just three years later).

It should also be said that Sade the philosopher and rhetorician was drawn to the use of dialogue by his love of theatre and experience as a playwright (by this time, he had written a number of conventional plays) and by his classical education in the Lycée Louis-le-Grand, the Jesuit-run school which he attended in Paris between the ages of ten and fourteen. Dialogue provides the philosopher with the question-and-answer format so well suited to the exposition of a balanced and reasoned argument. Dialogue allows Sade to manipulate our intellectual sympathies, and structurally the piece resembles a comic music-hall duet with the priest acting the part of straight man. The Dying Man is thus able to meet every one of the priest's objections with powerful logic and rhetorical force, there are amusing ironies, and a dénouement worthy of the best stage farces.

The Dying Man expresses Sade's own atheistic view that there is nothing after death. It is easy to overlook the shock-value of atheism in eighteenth-century Catholic France, when even the free-thinking authors of the *Encyclopedia*, Diderot and d'Alembert, felt obliged to condemn it in public: 'The most tolerant of men will not disagree that the judiciary has the right to suppress those who dare to profess atheism, and to put them to death even, if there is no other way of delivering society from it [. . .] If it may punish those who do harm to a single individual, it doubtless has just as much right to punish those who do harm to an entire society, in denying that there is a God [. . .] A man of this sort can be considered the enemy of all the rest.'[2] In contrast, Sade's bravery and candidness are admirable. In a letter to his wife, Sade declares that he would defend Baron d'Holbach's *System of Nature* (1770) 'to the point of martyrdom if necessary' (letter composed end November 1783). As all of Sade's correspondence was cen-sored by the authorities, outright expressions of support for atheistic philosophers carried considerable risks.

The Dying Man compares the reasoned basis of atheism to the pride at the root of theism: 'all the other theories are of pride's composition, this one alone is of reason's.' In writing these words, Sade doubtless has in mind the anthropocentricity of Christians determined to place Man at the centre of the universe. 'The flame of reason' led the forward march of all Enlightenment philosophies, inspiring the work of Voltaire, Diderot and Montesquieu among others. Sade dares to go fur-ther than these free-thinkers, in taking the rationalism of Enlightenment thought to its logical conclusion, dismissing not

only the medieval superstitions of religion but the very existence of God, which even atheistic philosophers such as
Diderot are reluctant to do under their own names. The deist
Voltaire was never able to reconcile the undeniable existence of
moral and physical evil on earth with the concept of an all-
powerful and benevolent deity. Nor could he satisfactorily
explain the paradox of God's determining human nature, while
allegedly leaving Man free to choose between right and wrong.

Sade both read and liberally plagiarized the atheistic French
materialists of his century, especially Baron d'Holbach and La
Mettrie. As we saw in the Introduction, his materialist notion
of nature has been primarily ascribed to d'Holbach's *System of
Nature*. La Mettrie and Helvétius have also been identified as
sources of his immoralism.[3] La Mettrie saw the human body
as a self-driven machine, perpetual motion making redun-
dant any idea of a motor. In the later works *Justine* and *Juliette*,
the libertines' attitudes to and manipulation of their victims'
bodies are strongly influenced by La Mettrie. If the human
body is a machine, it is simply a collection of pumps and
pipes that can be dismantled and sometimes even reassembled.
But for Sade, the body-machine is above all the site and
source of sexual pleasure, an emphasis missing from the work
of other eighteenth-century materialists. For the editor of
Sade's complete works in French, Annie Le Brun, it is,
indeed, Sade's unique contribution to modernity to have
brought the sexed body back into philosophy, a view that
runs counter to the structuralist emphasis on the purely linguistic nature of the writing, but which has gained some
ground among scholars since the 1980s.

When the priest falls back on the desperate and somewhat
circular argument that one must believe in something, so why
not in a theory of eternal punishment or reward, Sade intro-
duces the notion of perpetual renewal comprehensible outside

of any divine transcendental scheme ('Nothing perishes in the world . . .'). This conception of a material infinity, which Sade borrows and extends from d'Holbach, is nevertheless strikingly modern. While infinity has been a philosophical concept for millennia, scientific and astronomical notions of a never-ending series or process did not appear until after the Renaissance, and even the mathematical use of the infinite series is still problematical today. In promoting theories of a material as opposed to an abstract or spiritual infinity, Sade's thinking is very much of its time.

In spite of the scientific basis of these theories, however, there is a strong personal ambivalence in the Sadeian view of nature: on the one hand, a fascination with nature's power and destructive capabilities, on the other, a hatred for the blindness of a nature apparently without purpose and, allied to this, a desire to best nature, to challenge its sovereignty in the universe. Somewhere between these two extremes is the Sadeian libertine's philosophical transformation of nature into a machine of perpetual rebirth, a substitute in the material world for the immortality of the soul promised by religion. Though certainly not spiritual, Sade's nature not only substitutes for immortality but is itself quasi-divine in character. In *Juliette*, the libertines apostrophize nature as if it were a deity, to be admired and respected, and yet to be rivalled and ultimately destroyed.

The other major philosophical influence discernible here, one which is closely related to materialism and which is another dominant Sadeian theme, is determinism. When the Dying Man disclaims all responsibility for either virtues or crimes, objecting that this is a choice he is not free to make, he is relying on the theory that the world, or nature, is everywhere subject to causal law, that every event in it has a cause; consequently, that every event that actually happens *has* to happen. Likewise, any event that does not happen *could not* have happened. The principle of determinism was held by many leading Enlightenment thinkers, including Hume, Mill, Hobbes and Locke, to be one of the most fundamental laws of nature. If, like Sade, we include human actions in the deterministic system, then no one could ever have acted other than he did, and, therefore, no one can be held morally responsible for his actions. Sade's libertines constantly reiterate their rejection of the very notion of crime, on the basis that all human behaviour serves nature's will. Some might consider such a view to be a *reductio ad absurdum* of scientific determinism, but it is wholly in character for Sade to carry the logic of current philosophical ideas to their ultimate and often shocking conclusion. The moral relativity of all actions which underpins the Sadeian narrative is repeatedly rehearsed by his libertines. At the same time, if crime does not exist, the depiction in fiction of all that is in nature cannot be considered criminal either. This is the message of the epigraph to *The New Justine* (1799), the final and highly obscene version of Sade's best-known libertine novel: 'One is not criminal for painting the strange tendencies inspired by nature.'

Determinism certainly furnishes Sade with all the excuses he needs for desires considered beyond the pale by his society. Once again, we may be struck by the intensely personal motivations of the Sadeian philosophy. A letter which Sade wrote to his wife from prison underlines this point. In this letter, Sade states explicitly that d'Holbach's *System of Nature* is the basis of his philosophy. Crudely summarized, Sade exploits what he sees as the logical conclusions of d'Holbach's essential argument that all is in nature and that therefore everything that occurs in nature serves nature's purpose – a way of justifying all actions, even murder. Although Sade denies ever having murdered anybody, he readily admits to the lesser crime of libertinism – but then, if he is a libertine, it is not he who is to blame but Mother Nature herself, since she alone determines everything that happens. This link between d'Holbach's materialist ideas and Sade's rejection of all personal responsibility is strongly implied in the juxtaposition of the two ideas in the letter. In a long paragraph on d'Holbach's book, a copy of which he asks his wife to send to him so that he may reread it, Sade rails against the inanities of religion and emphasizes the workings of Nature without any primary cause. In a final paragraph, he then turns to his own character and situation. This letter, he jokes, will probably prolong his stay in prison, yet this would be a waste of time, 'for were they to leave me here for another ten years they would not see one whit of improvement [. . .]' After rehearsing all his virtues (honesty, sensitivity, compassion, charity, love of his wife, children, blood relatives and friends), the Marquis continues: 'As for my vices, much given to uncontrollable anger, extreme in everything, a profligate imagination when it comes to morals the likes of which the world has never seen, atheist to the point of fanaticism, in two words let me say it once again: either kill me or take me as I am, for I shall never change'. (Letter to Madame de Sade, late November 1783; translated by Richard Seaver)

The candid nature of Sade's list of his vices leads one to think that he did indeed believe that he also possessed the virtues he lays claim to. In any event, the main theme of his self-assessment is clearly a deterministic or fatalistic one: if there is no God to hold us responsible for our actions, and if the inexorable and amoral machine of Nature alone decides men's characters and therefore their behaviour, then he cannot be blamed for being who he is.

Whether Sade actually believed that there could be no such

thing as crime is debatable. On the one hand, the Jesuit-trained thinker loved to play devil's advocate, and it is certainly not implausible to regard such arguments as the Dying Man's as little more than an intellectual game. At the very least, Sade's accounts of the bloody revolutionary years in correspondence suggest strong opposition to the death penalty, which he viewed as a crime sanctioned by the state. On the other hand, there is undoubtedly an implicit plea in such passages for greater sympathy from the agencies of the law towards those like him who have been locked up for actions (sodomy, whipping) which he refuses to view as criminal since they are prompted by instincts that are inborn. (The extract from an earlier letter to his wife, dated February 1781, which was discussed in the previous chapter, is similarly self-justificatory in theme.)

At the very least one can say that Sade's text recognizes the fatality of the criminal instinct in Man, accepts that human nature has a dark side, and rejects the guilt that religion ascribes to Man for it: 'We are the pawns of an irresistible force . . .' In fact, as others have recognized, there is an inconsistency in the argument that runs throughout Sade's work and which makes his philosophy scandalous for some but radical for others: it is not reason, Sade suggests, but passion that determines our every thought and our every action.

Sade's writing style is wholly in keeping with his materialist vision of the world as unpoetic and unspiritual. There are no dazzling metaphors, only hackneyed images like the 'hornet' analogy, and as an evocation of feminine beauty in the closing lines, we must make do with a banal commonplace, 'lovelier than the light of day'. Such stereotypes are a common feature of Sade's language. He refuses to transcend the here and now, paying little attention to the verticality of a poetic imagery that attempts to link the body with a soul or the earth with a heaven, and channelling instead all his energy into the horizontal chain of prose, the linearity of which also offers the most efficient and most direct means of communicating his thought to the reader. Sentences are therefore syntactically well crafted, carefully constructed around rhetorical oppositions ('virtue' versus 'crime', 'corrupted' versus 'corrupt', for instance), and display a pleasing sense of rhythm (note the use of the ternary or three-part phrase throughout, most effectively in the coda to the piece). Both formally and thematically, *The Dialogue between a Priest and a Dying Man* is a skilful and original piece of work that foreshadows the great outpouring of radical writing to come.

$$\textbf{3}$$

SEX-THERAPY, SADEIAN STYLE

The close links between writing and eroticism are graphically illustrated in advice given by Juliette to Madame de Donis on the most effective path to self-knowledge. Although this passage apparently concerns female sexuality, the advice given here clearly applies to either sex.

Go a whole fortnight without lewd occupations, divert yourself, amuse yourself at other things; for the space of those two weeks rigorously bar every libertine thought from your mind. At the close of the final day retire alone to your bed, calmly and in silence; lying there, summon up all those images and ideas you banished during the fasting period just elapsed, and indolently, languidly, nonchalantly fall to performing that wanton little pollution by which nobody so cunningly arouses herself or others as do you. Next, unpent your fancy, let it freely dwell upon aberrations of different sorts and of ascending magnitude; linger over the details of each, pass them all one by one in review; assure yourself that you are absolute sovereign in a world grovelling at your feet, that yours is the supreme and unchallengeable right to change, mutilate, destroy, annihilate any and all the living beings you like. Fear of reprisals, hindrances you have none: choose what pleases you, but leave nothing out, make no exceptions; show consideration to no one whomsoever, sever every hobbling tie, abolish every check, let nothing stand in your way; leave everything to your imagination, let it pursue its bent and content yourself to follow in its train, above all avoiding any precipitate gesture: let it be your head and not your temperament that commands your fingers. Without your noticing it, from among all the various scenes you visualize one will claim your attention more energetically than the others and will so forcefully rivet itself in your mind that you'll be unable to dislodge it or supplant it by another. The idea, acquired by the means I am outlining, will dominate you, captivate you; delirium will invade your senses, and thinking yourself actually at work, you will discharge like a Messalina. Once this is accomplished, light your bedside lamp and write out a full description of the abomination which has just inflamed you, omitting nothing that could serve to aggravate its details; and then go to sleep thinking about them. Reread your notes the next day and, as you recommence your operation, add everything your imagination, doubtless a bit weary by now of an idea which has already cost you fuck, may suggest that could heighten its power to exacerbate. Now turn to the definitive shaping of this idea into a scheme and as you put the final touches on it, once again incorporate all fresh episodes, novelties, and ramifications that occur to you. After that, execute it, and you will find that this is the species of viciousness which suits you best and which you will carry out with the greatest delight. My formula, I am aware, has its wicked side but it is infallible, and I would not recommend it to you if I had not tested it successfully.

Juliette

There are many instances in the libertine novels of an intended humour that takes a variety of different forms: satire, parody, and black comedy are regular features. However, the reader will often encounter passages whose comical effects are probably unintentional. For example, there are numerous descriptions of sexual prowess and genital size, the excessive character of which seems ridiculous rather than arousing. Humorous responses to Sade are by no means new – the nineteenth-century English writer Swinburne and his friends roared with laughter as they read *Justine* aloud to each other.

Similarly, the modern reader may well find the adolescent earnestness of this passage amusing – an effect that, in this case, the author cannot have intended. Nevertheless, the passage deserves our attention, in that it throws an interesting light on conscious and unconscious attitudes to eroticism within the Sadeian text.

While Juliette's advice appears to offer a foolproof method of finding sexual satisfaction, underlying it is the anxiety, universal in Sade, that one's desires are ultimately unachievable, which is why Sade's libertines are constantly searching for new experiences and new thrills, why perversions multiply ceaselessly and become ever more extreme. The principal object of this never-ending quest is the female body, which the male libertines are drawn to penetrate and dissect, peeling off its layers like an onion, as if satisfaction were somehow located at its most profound and hidden levels. This quest is, of course, doomed to failure, which is perhaps why the libertine so often returns to the predictability of masturbation, which provides the nearest thing to total satisfaction of one's most secret desires.

In the twenty-first century, however, even masturbation may not be morally innocent, and this extract raises an important issue that all of Sade's critics, whether sympathetic or hostile, are obliged to confront. Essentially, the critical debate can be crudely summarized as follows: in one camp are those, like Andrea Dworkin and Roger Shattuck, who want to put Sade on trial as the author of a pornography that leads its consumers to act out the sexual perversions he depicts, and in the opposite camp are those like the structuralist Roland Barthes who completely divorce literature from reality, reading the scenarios of Sade's fiction as safely distant from the moral questions that would arise, were these to take place in the real world.

In fact, this passage undermines both positions. While

modern computer-based auto-erotic activities cannot be assumed not to have involved the abuse of others in their production (child pornography is an obvious example here), it would be hard to argue that recourse to the imagination alone is in any way morally reprehensible. At the same time, a purely literary reading of passages like this where writing and the body are inextricably linked seems inadequate. Sade must inevitably be recalling his dependence on writing in the isolation of his prison cell for vicarious sexual pleasure: is not Juliette's 'darkened room' an extension of the writer's cell? This short scene may in this sense be viewed as a microcosm of what has been described as Sade's 'prison literature'.

The crucial importance of the *imagination* in all erotic activity which this scene underlines appears time and time again both in Sade's fictions and his non-fictional writings. The accompanying notion of self-discovery, of the vital need to be aware of what we really want sexually, but perhaps emotionally and psychologically, too, suggests a philosophy of meditation and of self-help that, despite a long tradition in the East, did not come to dominate Western culture until the twentieth century. It is not inconceivable that Sade had access to this tradition – his library was vast and included works on the cultural practices of many countries – but this seems unlikely, given the relative insularity of the East at this time, in which case, the presence of such ideas in his text would be testimony to the originality of his thinking on eroticism.

Above all, perhaps, this extract drives home the message that Sade's libertine fiction is, first and last, the work of the imagination and no more dangerous than the mind of the person reading it. On this level, it has a unique contribution to make to an understanding of sexual fantasy, including its potential dangers. Firstly, Sade offers his reader a fictional representation of the imaginary that underpins all eroticism, hence the excess and implausibility of many of the perversions depicted. As the libertines are forever saying, it is the imagination that is the ultimate source of sexual pleasure. Secondly, when we read Sade and perhaps find ourselves aroused by certain passages, we confirm for ourselves both the erotic power of language and the links between sexual desire and its representation in writing and other media.

The following extract from a letter written by the Marquis to his wife from prison also deals with issues of auto-eroticism, but this time in a directly personal context. It illustrates Sade's use of codes and allusive references to evade the censor. Both Sade and his wife used code words. Here, 'vanille' stands for aphrodisiacs, while 'manille' represents Sade's peculiarly mechanical method of masturbation. The 'bow' is Sade's penis and the 'arrow' is sperm.

> To Madame de Sade
> I know full well that vanille causes overheating and that one should use manille in moderation. But what do you expect? When that is all one has – when one is reduced to these two items for one's source of pleasure! [. . .] One good hour in the morning for five manilles, artistically graduated from 6 to 9, a good half hour in the evening for three more, these last being smaller – no cause for alarm there, I should think; that seems more than reasonable; besides, when that is what you are used to, no one is any the worse the wear for it – and verily it gets the job done. I challenge someone to come up with anything better – and furthermore, I defy anyone to tell me that I haven't learnt something from being in Vincennes. What's more, I must say to you that whatever you lose in one area you more than make up for in another, 'tis like the person who is burning down the right side of his house and building it up on the left. For on the side that is not burning – 'tis a truly exemplary piece of wisdom, this – sometimes three months in truth, nor is it because the bow is not taut – oh, don't worry on that score, it is everything you could hope for as far as rigidity goes – but the arrow refuses to leave the bow

and that is the most exasperating part – because one wants it to leave – lacking an object one goes slightly crazy – and that doesn't help matters in the least – and 'tis for this reason I tell you that prison is bad, because solitude gives added strength only to ideas, and the disturbance that results therefrom becomes all the greater and ever more urgent.

But I've already made up my mind about the stubborn refusal of this arrow to leave the bow, all the more so because when, ultimately, it does cleave the air – 'tis veritably an attack of epilepsy – and no matter what precautions I may take I am quite certain that these convulsions and spasms, not to mention the physical pain, can be heard as far as the Faubourg St Antoine – you had some inkling of this at La Coste – well, I can tell you 'tis now twice as bad, so you can judge for yourself. In consequence thereof, when you take everything into consideration, there is more ill than good, so I'll stick with my manille, which is mild and has none of the above painful side effects. – I wanted to analyse the cause of this fainting spell, and believe that 'tis because of the extreme thickness – as if one tried to force cream out of the very narrow neck of a bottle or flask. That thickness inflates the vessels and tears them. That being so, the common wisdom is – the arrow ought to leave the bow more often – to which I agree most wholeheartedly – the only problem being, it simply doesn't want to – and to try to hold it back when it doesn't want to leave literally gives me such vapors that I think I'm dying.

Marquis de Sade: Letters from Prison

The 'Vanilla and Manilla' letter, written in late 1784 is remarkable for the explicitness but also for the simplicity and precision with which Sade describes to his wife his sexual activities in prison. Sade appears to have indulged in 'manille' several times a day with the aid of a number of specially made dildos which his devoted wife helped to procure for him. These dildos were designed for anal penetration.

This letter offers a counterweight to Juliette's prescription for sexual bliss. Sexual deprivation and solitude, when enforced for long periods of time as in Sade's own case, do not necessarily lead to sexual nirvana. He had already suffered seven years of imprisonment when he was transferred from Vincennes to the Bastille several months before the writing of this letter. In the cold half-light of his cell in the ironically named Liberty Tower of the Bastille, Sade's high sex-drive found expression only in auto-erotic activities that seldom resulted in orgasm, and which, even when they did, ended painfully. (The Marquis most likely suffered from a sexual irregularity, probably a venereal disease or prostate infection, which caused him considerable difficulty in ejaculating. He therefore had recourse to anal masturbation, partly as a substitute for penile ejaculation.) If anyone should doubt the overpowering grip of sexual desire on the Marquis, one single statistic may help convince: with his usual mania for counting, Sade recorded the number of his anal masturbations, which amounted to 6,536 in the space of only two and a half years.

The 'crisis', when it did come, resembled a type of epileptic fit. Some of Sade's biographers, notably Francine du Plessix Gray, believe that his masochistic tendencies were secretly satisfied by the pain he experienced during climax, and indeed his fictional works lend some support to this theory: many of the libertines themselves throw epileptic-type fits when ejaculating and such experiences appear to connote the paradoxical mix of pain and pleasure that defines masochism.

Despite the letter's complaining tones, the letter-writer cannot resist a certain amount of bragging, veiled in an apparently objective analysis of his condition – his sperm is 'thick' and 'like cream', the 'bow' is certainly 'taut'. Such details are evidence of both Sade's sexual focus and his egocentrism. Practically all of his letters, whether to his wife or to others such as his lawyer, reflect a self-obsession and self-dramatization – exemplified here in the complaint, 'I think I'm dying.'

Such melodramatic exclamations may well in some degree afflict all long-term prisoners, but unlike those detained under modern penal systems, the Marquis had no knowledge of when, if ever, he would be released. This uncertainty was a source of the greatest torment for a man who considered himself innocent of any crime and made continual but unsuccessful efforts to obtain his freedom.

The notion that imprisonment is harmful because it 'gives added strength only to ideas' is another leitmotif of the correspondence. What Sade seems to be saying is that when one is deprived of the freedom to express oneself physically and, above all, sexually, pent-up and frustrated desires can give rise to unhealthy and even dangerous thoughts. In particular, it is clear from other letters of this period that Sade missed having sex with his wife – 'lacking an object one goes slightly crazy' – who, he complained, did not visit him often enough. He had even, on one occasion, asked her to send him a piece of her clothing, most probably for masturbatory purposes.

The disturbance resulting from such deprivation could obviously be psychologically and emotionally injurious to the individual concerned. The dangers of sexual repression alluded to here by Sade prefigure Freud's thinking more than a century later. On the other hand, one might conjecture, as many critics have done, that the vast outpouring of narratives in which Sade found some release would not have occurred if he had not been incarcerated for twenty-seven years of his adult life. The enforced solitude and deprivation of a prison cell, in other words, led Sade to create a fantasy world of sexual adventure in which he might, through his fictional characters, vicariously experience the pleasure of both the intellect and the senses, a pleasure felt initially at least from the conjuring up of mental images in his writer's imagination. In fact, this passage does not so much contradict the premises of

Juliette's 'darkened room' as explain and complement them: what Sade discovered during those long years in prison was that the proper place of the erotic is not the body but the mind.

4

DESPOT OR DEMOCRAT?

'Won over to the principles Machiavelli set so clearly forth,' the Minister continued, 'I have for a long time had the profound conviction that individuals can be of no account to the politician; as machines, men must labor for the prosperity of the government they are subordinated to, never should the government be concerned for the welfare of the public. Every government that interests itself in the governed is weak; there is but one sort of strong government, and it considers itself everything and the nation nothing. Whether there are a few more or less slaves in a State does not matter; what does, is that their bondage weigh onerously and absolutely upon a people, and that the sovereign be despotic. Rome tottered feebly along in the days when Romans insisted upon governing themselves; but she became mistress of the world when tyrants seized authority; all the power resides in the sovereign, thus must we behold the thing, and since this power is merely moral so long as the people are physically the stronger, only by an uninterrupted series of despotic actions can the government assemble the force it needs: until such time as it commands all the real power, it will exist in an ideal sense only. When we are eager to gain the upper hand over others, we must little by little accustom them to seeing in us something which is actually not there; otherwise, they'll only see us for what we are, and this will regularly and inevitably be to our detriment . . .'

'It has always seemed to me,' Clairwil remarked, 'that the art of governing men is the one that demands more trickery, more duplicity, and more fraudulence than any other.'

'Perfectly true,' Saint-Fond assented, 'and the reason therefor is simple: there is no governing human beings unless you deceive them. To deceive them, you must be false. The enlightened man will never allow himself to be led about by the end of his nose, hence you must deprive him of light, keep him in darkness if you would steer him; none of this is possible without duplicity.'

[. . .] in a totally corrupt world there is never any danger being more rotten than one's neighbors; rather, [duplicity] is there to assure oneself of the whole sum of felicity and ease which virtue would procure us in a moral society. But the mechanism that directs government cannot be virtuous, because it is impossible to thwart every crime, to protect oneself from every criminal without being criminal too; that which directs corrupt mankind must be corrupt itself; and it will never be by means of virtue, virtue being inert and passive, that you will maintain control over vice which is ever active: the governor must be more energetic than the governed: well, if the energy of the governed simply amounts to so many crimes threatening to be unleashed, how can you expect the energy of the governor to be anything different? what are legally prescribed punishments if not crimes? and what excuses them? the necessity of governing men.

Juliette

The despotic political philosophy expressed in this relatively short dissertation by the diabolical Saint-Fond, one of the two wickedest male libertines in Sade's epic novel *The Story of Juliette* (1799), is typical of all such pronouncements on politics in the anonymous fiction. The essence of this philosophy, as in so many other areas of Sadeian thought, is *cynicism*.

Turning all traditional values and moral standards on their heads, the minister Saint-Fond declares himself to be a disciple of Machiavelli, and, indeed, appears here to espouse the main principles of Machiavelli's political credo, as set out in his best-known work, *The Prince* (1513), a handbook on the exercise of power which advises how a prince might achieve and retain supreme power in a state by entirely ruthless and amoral means. These principles can be summarized as follows.

A successful ruler must eschew traditional Christian virtues such as honesty or clemency, and provided he appears to observe conventional standards of morality and decency, he can act solely in accordance with his own interests:

> A prince should certainly try to be good and should shun vices which might make him so unpopular that he would be overthrown, but it is better to practise vices which will preserve his position than virtues which will destroy it. It is, for example, dangerous to be too generous since it can lead the prince into poverty.[4]

A prince, advised Machiavelli in what has been described as 'probably the most reviled and most emulated passage in all [his] works',[5] was 'often obliged, for the sake of maintaining his state, to act contrary to humanity, charity and religion'.[6]

Above all, the sovereign should ensure that he has enough force at his disposal to establish and maintain power.

Saint-Fond's speech certainly rings with Machiavellian tones: the emphasis on duplicity and deception, the need to keep one's true intentions hidden, 'accustoming people to seeing in us something which is actually not there', the subordination of the populace to the interests of strong government, the essential function of despotism in securing power, and the 'necessity of governing men' as a complete justification for the monarch's crimes. Furthermore, the reference to Rome's weakness recalls Machiavelli's condemnation of Scipio's clemency and of the disastrous behaviour of some of the later Roman emperors.[7]

By the time of the Enlightenment, Machiavelli's political philosophy was found less shocking in the Protestant countries of Europe than in the previous two centuries, mainly as a result of increasing secularism. In Catholic France, however, the dubious morality of his thought would still have been considered beyond the pale by the Church, though political leaders probably read him in private. For Sade's contemporaries, then, the apparent advocacy of a Machiavellian line may well have seemed quite radical. On the other hand, the 1790s were times of great instability, and radical ideas of every complexion were a permanent feature of the political landscape. Sade had clearly read *The Prince* and was doubtless impressed by its arguments and rhetoric, but respect for Machiavelli's rhetorical gifts and even sympathy with some of his ideas does not necessarily equate to wholesale intellectual and psychological conviction. Is this passage really intended as a serious endorsement, on the author's part, of Machiavellian *Realpolitik*, or is a satirical intention to be read between the lines? *Juliette* was written towards the end of a decade which had seen its fair share of Machiavellian figures. As we observed in our introduction, Sade loved to play the devil's advocate, especially in the fiction where he could do so with impunity.

Apart from the passage's Machiavellian aspects, there are also echoes of eighteenth-century materialism in Saint-Fond's description of men as machines. The modern reader might be tempted to see an analogy here with Marx's analysis of the capitalist machine and its alienation of workers, and it is not inconceivable that Sade was himself striking a satirical note in pushing materialist thinking to its logical extreme. Sade knew better than most what it was like to be treated like an object during his long periods of imprisonment.

It is the final paragraph, especially, however, that reads most plausibly as political parody or satire. We must not forget that Sade's contemporary reader would very likely have shared the ex-Marquis's own vivid memories of recent events under the Terror, criminal acts that were justified in terms similar to Saint-Fond's. Sade was a strong opponent of all laws that carried long prison sentences, which, through personal experience, he knew to be ineffective in reforming the prisoner, and especially of the death penalty, the horrific and bloody reality of which he had witnessed on numerous occasions from his window during a spell of detention at Picpus (the guillotine had been moved there from the Place de la Révolution, now the Place de la Concorde, when the stench of blood became unbearable). He himself had narrowly escaped the guillotine thanks to a simple bureaucratic error. Suspected of 'political moderation', he had been arrested and imprisoned in December 1793, and was awaiting execution along with many other ex-aristocrats. When his name was finally called out from the list of those to be executed, he had been moved to another prison and was marked as absent. He was released soon afterwards, following the fall and execution of Robespierre. Given Sade's personal experience of what he regarded as state-sponsored murder, it is unthinkable that Sade could have shared Saint-Fond's sanctioning of 'governmental crimes'.

While he may have been horrified by revolutionary fanaticism, Sade had no reason either to regret the passing of a monarchy that had not baulked at the use of summary methods of justice when it suited. The speech relies on a vocabulary of feudalism – 'slaves', 'bondage', 'sovereign', 'despotic', 'tyrants' – that could only have had an ironic charge in the 1790s, but Saint-Fond's language generally is sufficiently ambiguous to be read as an ironic attack, as much on Jacobin extremism as on the excesses of the *ancien régime*. The sophism that governments are required to commit crimes in order to impede criminal behaviour among the people may be interpreted broadly, therefore, as a cynical comment on the entire political history of eighteenth-century France. The 'totally corrupt world' in which one can be rotten with impunity seems a fairly accurate description of life in France since the reign of Louis XIV – an observation Sade's narrator makes in a work composed well before the Revolution:

> The extensive wars wherewith Louis XIV was burdened during his reign, while draining the State's treasury and exhausting the substance of the people, none the less contained the secret that led to the prosperity of a swarm of those bloodsuckers who are always on the watch for public calamities, which, instead of appeasing, they promote or invent so as, precisely, to be able to profit from them more advantageously.
>
> *The 120 Days of Sodom*, written in the Bastille in the 1780s

The 120 Days is, on one level, a savage satire of the corruption that was endemic in France at the beginning of the eighteenth century and that would continue throughout the reigns of Louis XV and Louis XVI. The novel opens with a clear denunciation of this corruption in the portrait of its four leading protagonists as free-booters whose wealth was built on warmongering. The corruption of individuals is hardly surprising, Sade here implies, when the state itself is morally corrupt.

The next passage appears to express a political stance that could not be further removed from the fictional Saint-Fond's. In this extract from a speech delivered by 'citizen Sade' during the revolutionary period, on 2 November 1792, we hear the voice of an ardent democrat. Does either passage represent the author's true political views?

Idea on the Method for the Sanctioning of Laws

You now ask which is the best method for sanctioning laws whilst retaining the sovereignty which you have received from nature, which despotism stole from you, and which you have just regained at the cost of your blood? This is what I propose as the quickest and most majestic means of giving the people that indispensable power of sanction without which there is no law for a free nation.

An initial letter will give notice to the mayors of the chief town of each canton of the French territory. As soon as they have received this, they will convene primary assemblies which will meet in the chief town of the canton. Following the wise precautions of our legislators, the proposed law will only then be sent to them in a second mailing. These magistrates of the people will read out the bill to the assembled people. Having been examined, discussed, and carefully studied by the collective mass of individuals that it will serve, this bill will then be accepted or rejected. In the former case, the messenger who has just brought it will immediately take it back, the will of the majority prevailing, and the bill will be promulgated. Should it only secure the support of a minority, your *députés* must immediately modify, suppress or recast it, and if they succeed in improving it, it should be presented a second time to the whole of France gathered together in the same way in all cantons of the various *départements*.

My translation

Following the Revolution, Sade had quickly become active in the meetings and activities of his local revolutionary committee. Indeed, Louis Sade, man of letters, as he described himself at this time, made something of a name for himself as an orator and, largely thanks to his rhetorical gifts, rose to the position of secretary of his section, the Section des Piques. In this polemical essay on the drafting and passing of laws, which was initially delivered as a speech to his local committee, Sade advocates one of the most democratic methods of government ever conceived. Some readers may find this surprising, coming from a former aristocrat. By 1792 when this speech was delivered, Sade had of course done his best to erase all vestiges of his aristocratic past. Most strikingly, though, this is the first time that Sade breaks explicitly with the principle of royal sovereignty.

In the opening paragraph, the speech is addressed to those

who, on 10 August 1792, had marched on the Tuileries in a new revolutionary fervour: 'MEN OF THE 10TH OF AUGUST, you were not afraid to drag the despot from his proud palace where tyrants would spill the blood of the people for the second time!' The Marseillais and Bretons who took part in this action had suffered some fatalities when fired on by the King's guard. In a single phrase, 'for the second time', Sade deftly reminds his audience that this was not the first instance of monarchical despotism at the Tuileries, where in the sixteenth century Charles IX had fired on Protestants from the same windows. Citizen Sade is thus at pains to align himself from the outset both with the ordinary people and the revolutionary cause. These sentiments, expressed less than three months after the event, could not have been more topical.

The principal argument of this essay is that all legislation put forward by the deputies should be scrutinized by the people in cantonal assemblies before being allowed to become law. Power delegated to a prince, a monarch or even an assembly, Sade maintains, is power usurped and open to abuse. The central idea here, then, is that popular sovereignty is indivisible. Sade wants to bypass any system of representative democracy according to which elected *députés* legislate in the people's name, and give the people a right of veto of all proposed laws. The essay expresses a fundamental mistrust of any form of delegation of power that was shared by both the *sans-culottes* and the more radical Jacobins. The views expressed here are also very close to those put forward by the ill-fated Marat, whom Sade purported to admire (although Gilbert Lély suggests that there may be an element of parody in this admiration of a man whom Lély describes as 'the most hideous vampire of the Revolution'[8]). Be that as it may, they certainly bear testimony to a general fear among the common people of the return of despotism, which Marat also shared.

Though difficult to put into practice, this method has to be the most democratic imaginable. Consequently, Sade's essay was very favourably received by the general assembly of the Section des Piques, who unanimously voted to have it printed and sent out to the other forty-seven Paris sections. This alone showed how much in tune Sade was with radical revolutionary thinking.

Sade's radical proposal is certainly an interesting idea and is the basis of all modern referenda. Sade here seems to espouse a genuine belief in the natural wisdom of common man which is completely out of tune with the cynical contempt for the masses expressed by fictional libertines like Saint-Fond. Is it a matter of Sade simply playing the revolutionary game, pushing the democratic ideal to its logical and absurd extreme, in other words, parodying the republican aims of the Revolution to the extent of demonstrating their essentially impractical, unrealizable nature, or must we accept that Sade the man and citizen and his fictional anti-heroes have polar opposite views?

The French critic Philippe Roger is convinced that Sade is actually a 'political minimalist', that he has no strong political sympathies with any particular faction. Sade's correspondence during the revolutionary years and his other political writings certainly express a degree of confusion in this area: 'Who am I at present,' he writes to his lawyer, Gaufridy, in 1791, 'aristocrat or democrat? Please tell me . . . as for me, I don't know any more' (5 December 1791). Like so many others, Sade was pulled in different directions. Although he had no love for a monarchy that had kept him in prison for so many years, psychologically and emotionally the ex-aristocrat was still anchored in the past. On the other hand, as we observed in an earlier chapter, Sade the life-long actor and dramatist was used to playing parts, a gift that he could call upon in the great theatre of

revolution just as easily as on the stage, and he never fully co-
incides with any of the roles he appears to play at this time.

The enigma of Sade's politics is beautifully captured in the
imaginary portrait by the early twentieth-century surrealist
artist Man Ray which is frequently reproduced in editions of
Sade's works. The portrait depicts an ageing and rotund Sade,
constructed out of the stones of the Bastille that kept him
locked up for a decade. By the end of his first long period of
imprisonment, Sade was hugely obese, having regularly con-
sumed large quantities of rich food with limited freedom to
exercise. But the meaning of Man Ray's painting has more to
do with the inscrutability of Sade on a political level. The
image perfectly expresses his complicity as an aristocrat with
the *ancien régime* to the extent that he is part of the very fabric
of the Bastille, symbol of its repressive power, and yet, at the
same time, it suggests his estrangement from and even outright hostility to an old order of monarchy that had treated
him so badly. Man Ray's Marquis fiddles while Paris burns.

This painting also has a self-consciously theatrical character,
suggested by the frame which emphasizes the representational
nature of the image. In this sense, the Marquis's inflated figure
is a self-avowed conceit, an exaggerated visual metaphor for
Sade's alleged historical role in the first act of the drama of
revolution. Days before the Bastille was stormed, Sade is said
to have harangued the street crowds from his cell, urging
them to rise up and revolt – perhaps the most theatrical of all
episodes in his very theatrical life.

In the theatre of revolution, Sade was to play many more
parts: rabble-rouser, citizen Sade, gifted orator and revolutionary magistrate, and although in all of these roles he
appeared to be an active supporter of the new republic, in the
end he cannot easily be fixed with any particular political
label. Responding along with many of his contemporaries to

events as they happened, Sade the man is a pragmatist, skilfully adapting his rhetoric to suit a changing public mood and in his anonymous fictions to please a readership that has come through those changes less idealistic, less polarized and more cynical than ever before.

5

LOUIS SADE, MAN OF LETTERS

To Intending Authors

[. . .] in urging you to embellish, I am forbidding you from wandering away from verisimilitude [. . .] no one expects you to be truthful but only convincing; to ask too much of you would be to limit the pleasure we expect from you. Don't replace the true, however, with the impossible; and let your inventions be well presented; you will not be pardoned putting your imagination in the place of truth, except when this is clearly done in order to ornament and dazzle. One never has the right to put things poorly, when one can say whatever one wishes. If, like Restif, you write only what everyone already knows, then don't bother to take up the pen; if, again like him, you turn out four volumes a month, you will find such productivity no compensation against familiarity. No one is forcing you to follow this career, but if you do, do it well. By all means, don't choose it simply as an aid to your existence; your work, then, will be impregnated with your needs; you will transmit your weakness to it; it will have hunger's pallor.

Avoid the affectation which comes with pointing out morals; this is not what one looks for in a novel. If the characters demanded by your plot are sometimes compelled to argue things out, let them always do so without pretentiousness, without seeming to have the purpose of doing so. The author should never make moral statements, only the characters – and they should never be allowed to do so unless the circumstances clearly make it necessary.

When you get to the dénouement, let it be natural, never con-
strained or trumped-up. I do not ask, as do the authors of the
Encyclopédie, that it conform to the reader's desire: what pleasure is
there for him, if he has guessed everything in advance?

[...]

Finally, I must reply to the reproach which was made to me when my
Aline et Valcour was published. My paintbrushes, it was said, used
colors that were too strong; I attributed traits to vice which were too
hateful. Do my critics want to know why? I do not wish to have vice
loved; unlike Crébillon [fils] and Dorat, I do not wish to undertake the
dangerous project of having women love those who deceive them. On
the contrary, I hope they would detest them; mine was the only way
of assuring that they will not be turned into dupes. In order to meet
with success in such an undertaking, I made those of my heroes who
were given over to vice so frightful that they could certainly inspire
neither pity nor love; by so doing, I acted more morally than those
who feel entitled to embellish them. [. . .] And let no one hold me
responsible for the story, *Justine*. I have never written such works and
surely I never shall. Only imbeciles or the wicked could, despite the
genuineness of my denials, still suspect or accuse me of being its
author. The most extreme scorn will henceforth be the unique arm
with which I shall fight their calumnies.

'Note on the Novel', from *Yale French Studies,* No. 35

Sade's *Idée sur les romans* ('Note [or 'Reflections'] on the Novel')
was composed as a preface to the short-story collection entitled
Crimes de l'amour, and published in 1799, just two years before
his arrest for the publication of *Justine*. In the final section of the
essay from which this extract is taken, Sade rather grandly offers
advice to those contemplating a career as a writer.

Earlier in the essay, Sade had reviewed the development of
the novel from classical times, via the troubadours of medieval
Europe to late sixteenth- and seventeenth-century Spain and
France, before evaluating leading novels of the eighteenth
century. The essay shows how well read Sade was and offers
some insight into his literary ideas.

Sade wished to be remembered, above all, as a man of let-ters, and the critical *Idée* genre, then very much in vogue, was another expression of this ambition.[9] (The *Idée* was a short essay designed to express thoughts on a specific subject. The genre all but disappeared in the nineteenth century.)

The Crimes of Love was a collection of eleven short stories, the only works of fiction published by Sade under his own name. These tales were largely conventional in style, contain-ing no obscene descriptions, although they shared some of the themes of the libertine novels (incest, libertinage and disaster). The eleven stories were chosen from more than fifty tales written in the 1780s during Sade's imprisonment in the Bastille. Originally, he had intended to publish a much larger collection in which humorous stories would alternate with tragic ones under the title *Tales and Fabliaux of the Eighteenth Century by a Provençal Troubadour*. However, the comic tales did not reach the public domain until 1926, when Maurice Heine published twenty-six of them. When he came to pub-lish *The Crimes*, Sade deliberately selected only 'sombre' tales for his collection, which may have been more in tune with the public's taste at the time for the Gothic novel (Matthew Lewis's *The Monk*, for example, was a runaway best-seller in England at the end of the eighteenth century, and a work for which Sade expressed qualified praise).

Sade is concerned here to stamp his critical authority on the literary scene. The very fact that he gives detailed advice to budding novelists stakes his claim as an experienced practi-tioner of the genre. The entire piece focuses not on prose generally, as one might expect in a preface to a collection of short stories, but exclusively on the novel.

The advice regarding verisimilitude harks back to a very long tradition in French literature of privileging believability over truthfulness. Racine in the seventeenth century had famously declared that 'truth is sometimes not believable'. Indeed, Racine's century was in some ways preoccupied with the gap between appearance and reality. What mattered was that a writer should be artful enough to make fiction appear factual. Sade, however, is not only pompous in remonstrating with other writers in this way, he is also guilty of not a little hypocrisy. His own libertine fictions, most of which had been written and published by the time he composed this essay, are replete with exaggerations and excesses of all kinds. Borrowing from the tradition of the moral tale, but also from the *roman noir* or Gothic novel, Sade's libertine novels *Justine* and *Juliette* have more in common with the dark fairy-tales of the brothers Grimm than with any other genre, while *Philosophy in the Boudoir* shares with both of these novels a strong tendency towards comic excess amidst the most horrific of scenes. On the other hand, this exhortation to be believable makes some sense in relation to those historical novels, *Adelaide of Brunswick, Princess of Saxony*, *The Secret History of Isabelle of Bavaria* and *The Marquise de Gange*, which Sade would write during 1812 and 1813, but which must have been years in the planning. The only fictions that Sade acknowledged as his, and which included these three works, were in fact those that could not be taxed with a lack of verisimilitude. Nevertheless, readers of the entire corpus will not miss the irony here.

Other rules prescribed in this passage are often not adhered to by Sade himself. For example, his injunction to would-be authors never to make moral statements does not chime well with his own tendency to do so in the numerous footnotes that accompany the text of *Juliette*. Sade's own dénouements are frequently far from 'natural'. The first two versions of *Justine*, for instance, may be said to pander to the desires of many readers (and especially the censors) in fabricating a completely implausible ending, according to which Juliette becomes a reformed character following her sister's tragic demise and determines to spend the rest of her days living a life of virtue behind the walls of a convent. The ultimate triumph of virtue at the end of a narrative which has insistently demonstrated the ubiquitous supremacy of vice is most likely a transparent piece of irony or else a cynical sop to the conventions of the time.

The essay had begun in a sober and restrained manner, but Sade's fiery temperament can scarcely contain itself when sensitive issues are touched upon, and attempts to maintain a tone of lofty, scientific objectivity give way at times to a desire to settle personal scores. The barb aimed here, for example, at Restif (or Rétif) de la Bretonne echoes an earlier paragraph in the essay, in which Sade had launched a vituperative and scathing attack on his contemporary. Restif, also the author of a number of pornographic novels in which incest is a favourite theme, had himself written an acerbic critique of 'the vivisectionist' Sade, whom he called 'Dsds'. In his four-volume popular novel *Monsieur Nicolas* (1794–7), Restif features the revolutionary hero Danton as reading the sadistic passages of *Justine* to excite himself before committing further acts of cruelty in the Terror. He also composed a novel provocatively entitled *L'Anti-Justine* (1798), allegedly an attempt to demonstrate that you can write about sex in an interesting way without recourse to the depictions of cruelty found in Sade's notorious works. Ironically, Restif manages to outdo Sade himself in his representations of sexual cruelty in this novel.

Sade's rather too insistent denial at the end of this extract of the authorship of *Justine*, which Restif had been most vociferous in attributing to him, is aimed specifically at Restif, implicitly castigated here as an 'imbecile' or a 'wicked' man.

The denial is, of course, disingenuous in the extreme. There is not the slightest doubt that Sade was the author of the book. Indeed, quite apart from the similarity of themes and style, the very first version of *Justine*, a short story entitled *The Misfortunes of Virtue*, was intended to be included in the collection. But at a time when Sade wished to establish his credentials as a bona fide man of letters (this, we remember, is the main purpose of the *Idée*), any association with the most infamous work of the eighteenth century was highly undesirable.

The enjoinder to would-be novelists not to choose the profession 'simply as an aid to your existence' is also hypocritical. Sade's decision to concentrate on writing novels in the 1790s rather than plays or short stories was in large part motivated by his desperate need for money. He had been released from captivity in 1790 without a sou to his name. His lands had been seized during the Revolution and there had been years of mounting debts, probably the result of bad management and neglect of the family properties. Both versions of *Justine* that were published during his lifetime (in 1791 and 1799), and the sequel *Juliette* were produced at the request of Sade's editor for 'well spiced' novels that would sell well. In fact, Sade never made much from these works, and indeed paid the price of his freedom for having written them.

The 'Note on the Novel', then, is an erudite and rhetorically interesting piece of writing that bears witness to Sade's literary aspirations, and expresses views with which he wished to be publicly associated, but its true value lies in documenting contemporary debates on the depiction of reality and the writer's role as a moralist, and in illuminating Sade's attitudes to these issues. In fact, when the essay is placed in the context of his anonymous writings, the real Sade emerges, as ever, from between the lines, a Sade who is far more inclined to infringe rules than to observe them. After all, his enduring reputation is based, not on the extent to which his work conforms or not to the conventional literary standards of the late eighteenth century, but on the extent to which this work is seen to subvert not only literary and artistic norms but moral codes and values. As the author and essayist Angela Carter points out, all art for Sade is quite simply 'the perpetual immoral subversion of the existing order'.[10]

6

LIBERTINAGE IN THEORY AND PRACTICE

Rules of the Libertines

In order to become a member of the predominantly male
libertine club, the Sodality of the Friends of Crime, Juliette is
required to agree to a number of conditions, among which are
the following:

> Far from alarming her, let the most extensive, the most sustained, the
> most crapulous libertinage become the basis of her most cherished
> occupations; if she lends an ear to Nature, she will discover that from
> her she has received very pronounced leanings, very violent ones,
> toward this sort of pleasure, and there being no grounds here for fear
> and fewer yet for restraint, she ought to indulge herself therein con-
> stantly: the more she fucks, the better she answers Nature's
> expectations of her. Nature is not to be outraged save by continence.
>
> *Juliette*

At this point in the text, the author appends the following
footnote:

> Almost all chaste women die young, or go mad, or become sickly and
> wither early away. Furthermore, they are all ill-natured, testy, for-
> ward, and rude; they are unbearable in society.

By the time she nears the end of her long adventure, Juliette has herself become an authority on libertinism to the extent that male libertines are curious to discover her opinions on the subject. In the following extract, Juliette's fellow female libertine, the witch and poisoner Durand, makes her own contribution to the debate:

'Juliette,' [Cornaro] asks me, 'what is your view? Is there any more divine passion in the world than lust?'

'I would venture to say that there is not; but lust must be carried to excess: in libertinage, he who applies curbs is a fool who denies himself all possibility of ever knowing what pleasure is.'

'Libertinage,' Durand put in, 'is a sensual aberrance which supposes the discarding of all restraints, the supremest disdain for all prejudices, the total rejection of all religious notions, the profoundest aversion to all ethical imperatives; and that libertine who has not attained this philosophical maturity, tossing back and forth between his desires' impetuousness and the bullying of his conscience, will be debarred from perfect happiness.'

Juliette

The key words in these two extracts are all superlatives: 'the most crapulous', 'the most extensive', 'the most sustained', 'the supremest disdain', 'the total rejection', 'the profoundest aversion'. Superlativity is semantically associated with both divinity and excess. Lust for the libertine is divine, allowing men to rival the gods. On earth, the Sadeian libertine can only approach divinity through excess. Thus, everything in the Sadeian universe is excessive, from the isolation of libertine retreats in the most inaccessible mountain eyries, to the consumption of superhuman quantities of food and wine, from the comic-book dimensions of male genitals, to the cruelty of methods devised for torturing and killing. All excesses are justified by nature, since, as the libertines are wont to tell their accomplices and even their victims, everything that naturally

occurs, including what some societies call crimes, must logically serve nature's plan. Excess means forever pushing the
boundaries of what is humanly (or inhumanly) possible,
searching for some lost dimension of sovereign power that
might make the human more than human.[11] Excess exceeds all
expectations, excess is that ever-moving line that the libertine
is impelled to keep transgressing, because *jouissance*[12] is only
possible in the transgression of norms and rules, physical, moral
and religious.[13]

Both Georges Bataille and Julia Kristeva have developed
theories of transgression that owe a considerable debt to Sade
and, at the same time, help to illuminate a fundamental feature
of Sadeian eroticism. In a discussion of the links between
reproduction and death in his principal theoretical work,
Eroticism, Bataille reminds us that, long before Freud, St
Augustine himself was only too aware of the proximity of the
sexual organs to the processes of bodily evacuation: 'Inter
faeces et urinam nascimur,' he declared, ('We are born
between faeces and urine').[14] For Bataille, the taboo and its
transgression are two sides of the same coin: as taboo sub-
stances that remind us of degeneration and death, urine and
faeces are repugnant, but, like all taboos, they are also fascinating, because they represent the challenge of transgression:

> To enjoy to the utmost the ecstasy, in which we lose ourselves in
> orgasm, we must always know what the borderline is: it is horror. [. . .]
> there is no form of repugnance that does not have an affinity with
> desire.[15]

Julia Kristeva has also developed a theory of transgression
which helps us to understand Sade's eroticization of the physically repugnant. Kristeva suggests that, in order to be
accepted into 'civilized' society, the individual is obliged to
repress some aspects of his or her sexuality. She calls these

aspects the 'abject', locating them especially in bodily functions involving the expulsion of waste products such as urine,
faeces, pus and menstrual blood. Like Bataille, Kristeva argues
that the shame that these products induce in the individual is
connected to a repressed eroticism.[16] These views of the role
of transgression and abjection in eroticism draw heavily on
Sade's work, in which the libertines are seen to derive their
greatest thrills from coprophilia (the eating of faeces and the
drinking of urine) as well as from the infringement of social
and sexual taboos in the raping of virgins, the sexualization of
children, sodomy with both sexes, and the violent dismemberment and reconstruction of their victims' bodies. In *The
120 Days of Sodom*, the four libertines practise all manner of
transgressive acts that are physically and/or morally repugnant, including the consumption of shit, which they also force
upon their victims.

Sadeian eroticism, however, is not confined to the transgressive use of bodily waste. The following brief passage offers
a particularly gruesome example of the use of violence to
transgress boundaries that are both physical and cultural. In a
process that uncannily foreshadows modern realignment sur-
gery for male-to-female transsexuals, the brutal transformation
of a boy into a girl challenges both the laws of nature and cultural perceptions of sex in relation to gender:

> After having sheared off the boy's prick and balls, using a red-hot iron
> he hollows out a cunt in the place formerly occupied by his genitals; the
> iron makes the hole and cauterises simultaneously: he fucks the
> patient's new orifice and strangles him with his hands upon discharging.
> *The 120 Days of Sodom*

The Sadeian libertine must be ready to transcend all limits,
without exception. This process of transcendence is itself
limitless, unending, because, like Sartre's existentialist hero,

Sadeian man is defined only by his actions, and is thus in a constant process of becoming. Fixity puts an end to the libertine's identity, draws a line beneath it so that it can be weighed, assessed, and ultimately found wanting, because the libertine quest which can never be satisfied is foreclosed. Fixity is failure, fixity is death. Virtue fixes Man with moral absolutes: purity, honour, probity, charity, love. Virtue is fixity, virtue is stagnation, virtue is weakness. Only vice transcends absolutes, breaks through limits, is ever-moving in search of new thrills to savour, fresh taboos to transgress. Vice is mobility, vice is energy, vice is strength.

The libertine desires to be nothing less than supreme, the most cruel, the most lascivious, the most criminal. Nothing less will do. Anything less will be deemed unacceptable, because less than perfect means inferior, and inferiority is weakness and subjection. Juliette's fatal error is to allow her libertine will to falter for one brief moment, revealing an imperfection that seals her death warrant, and she is forced to flee Saint-Fond's wrath. This moment of weakness is Juliette's human error, the Sadeian equivalent of the Shakespearean hero's tragic flaw. Moments such as this might be taken as evidence in Sade's text of an underlying critique of the libertine philosophy.

Although libertinism is a principally male occupation, women are not only not excluded from the libertine club, they are despised if they are not sexually free. The authorial footnote to the first passage above expresses Sade's contempt for chastity: women should be as sexually active as men, indeed, they need to be so if men are to be free to take their pleasure whenever they desire.

Female libertines must, however, conform in every sense to the male model of libertinage, or else they run the risk of becoming the universal female victim. In this respect, Juliette is an exemplary female libertine. In fact, Juliette shares all the behavioural traits and sexual preferences of her male sodomist associates, to the extent that only the lack of the appropriate anatomical equipment prevents her from conforming exactly to that model. In her sexual attraction to other women, for example, she shares the preference of her male libertine friends for the female posterior and penetrates the anus with the aid of dildos.

If her active sexual performances are intrinsically masculine, so too is her status as passive sexual object. Again, sodomy is the order of the day: 'They devour me, but in the Italian style: my ass becomes the unique object of their caresses [. . .] they [. . .] behave for all the world as if they are unaware I am a woman' (*Juliette*). In a more general sense, Juliette displays attitudes and characteristics more recognizably male than female: she is promiscuous, goal-orientated and prioritizes reason over emotion, a woman defined in terms of male fantasies and objectives.

Libertinage in Sade's world is an essentially male activity, and those few female characters who achieve libertine status do so by assuming the sexual and psychological perspectives of their male companions.

Theory Put to the Test

His glittering eyes fall once again upon my daughter; his erection is that of a maniac; he seizes Marianne, has her pinioned, and encunts her.

'By God,' he cries, 'this little creature makes my head spin, damn me if 'tis not true. What do you mean to do with her, Juliette? You are not the sentimental fool, you are not the idiot to have feelings for this loathsome spawn of your abominable husband's testicle; so sell her to me. Sell me the slut, Juliette, I wish to buy her from you; let's both soil ourselves, you in the pretty sin of vending me your child, I in the still more rousing one of paying you only in order to assassinate her. Yes, Juliette, yes, let's assassinate your daughter' – and here he finished wiping his prick and nodded toward it, gleaming and purple – 'consider, if you will, how this idea inflames my senses. Stay, Juliette, have yourself fucked before you pronounce, answer me not till you have a pair of pricks in your body.'

Crime holds no terrors for anyone when in the act of fucking; and one must always ponder its attractions when swimming in tides of sperm. Pricks penetrate me, I am fucked; a second time Noirceuil inquires to what purpose I wish to put my daughter.

'O villainous soul!' I cry, loosing discharge upon discharge, 'star of perfidy, your ascendant places all else in eclipse, smothers all else in me save the longing for crime and infamy . . . With Marianne do you what you please, whoreson knave,' say I, beside myself, 'she is yours.'

No sooner does he hear these words than he decunts, takes hold of the poor child in his two wicked hands, and hurls her, naked, into the roaring fire; I step forward and second him; I too pick up a poker and thwart the unhappy creature's natural efforts at escape, for she thrashes convulsively in the flames; we drive her back, I say; we are being frigged, both of us, then we are being sodomized. Marianne is being roasted alive; and we go off to spend the rest of the night in each other's arms, congratulating each other upon the scene whose episodes and circumstances complement a crime which, atrocious perhaps, is yet, in our shared opinion, too mild.

'So tell me now,' said Noirceuil, 'is there anything in the world to match the divine pleasures crime yields? Is there anything that can compete with the criminal humor? Beyond the criminal sensation is there anything that produces such vibrations in us?'

'No, my friend, not to my knowledge.'

'Then let us live in crime forever; and may nothing in all Nature ever succeed in converting us to different principles. He is not a man to be envied who, smitten by remorse, undertakes the equally baneful and imprudent and needless retreat; for, irresolute, pusillanimous in his acts, he will be no happier in his new career than he was in the one he renounces. Happiness is dependent upon energetic principles, and there can be none for him who wavers all his life.'

Juliette

This scene comes near the end of Juliette's long narrative of her adventures, and represents a heightening of the horror in anticipation of the shocking dénouement, in which Justine, too, is sacrificed to the libertines' whims. Marianne, Juliette's lovely seven-year-old daughter, has already been raped by the appalling Noirceuil. Having committed numerous atrocities on children, including the sodomizing and murder of his own son, Noirceuil here asks the mother's permission to murder Marianne in turn.

Notwithstanding this scene's transgressive charge, as always with instances of extreme sex and violence in Sade, one must beware of a naïve literal reading. The gruesome murder of Marianne is intended neither as a realistic event nor even as the main point of the scene. Only pages before, Juliette had referred to her child as 'my poor Marianne', implying some degree of compassion. Noirceuil's request in this light takes on the character of a challenge: what matters is Juliette's response, not the act itself. The question is whether Juliette is a true libertine (one who sacrifices all else to sexual pleasure). Noirceuil's proposal is simply an instance of the philosophy of libertinism (as expressed in Sade's text), taken to its logical extreme. The killing by a mother of her own child, in the absence of any mental imbalance on her part, is perhaps the most horrific crime imaginable, partly because it is perceived as against nature. Sade's fictions, however, repeatedly hammer home the lesson that nature in general and human nature in particular are inimical to the very concept of crime. Many of the passages on nature in Sade read as a merciless satire of Rousseau's romantic view of nature (what Noirceuil here obliquely refers to as sentimentality). Rousseau's love of nature was a key feature of his philosophy. For him, urban life was corrupting, whereas the countryside fostered man's innate goodness. Happiness, for Rousseau, could be found only in nature's bosom. This naïvely sentimental view of nature also expresses itself in Rousseau's portrayal of nature's mysterious influence on the soul, inspiring strong, positive emotions in his fictional characters. In sharp contrast to this sentimentality, the storms and volcanoes of Sade's fictional world merely incite his libertines to greater cruelty (see Chapter 7). Human nature itself is always portrayed in Sade as intrinsically selfish and cruel. What better illustration of the naturalness of cruelty than infanticide? As Dolmancé declares in *Philosophy in the Boudoir*, any man with an erection is a tyrant.

Noirceuil's erection is seen here as a symptom of a madness ('maniac') that is the very opposite of reason. 'The flame of reason', brandished with such pride by so many Enlightenment philosophers, has no currency here. For Juliette, it is the flame of the passions that drives men and women alike. It is not insignificant that Juliette yields to Noirceuil's demand when she is in the throes of sexual ecstasy.

Here, of course, the 'flame' metaphor takes on a more literal meaning. Marianne's death by burning suggests the notion of sacrifice. Fire and the divine have long been associated in human culture, fire serving principally as a means of appeasing an angry divinity or of paying homage to the divinity in order to secure its continued protection. The sacrifice of the life of a child by a mother is the greatest sacrifice imaginable, perhaps even greater than that of one's own life, while the sacred status of libertinism for its followers is as absolute a creed as any religion. Mirroring primitive man's attitude to his chosen divinity, the libertines have an uneasy relationship with fire, as with nature in general: admired by them as a sign of nature's power, fire is at the same time respected, especially for its destructive potential.

Fire is a recurrent cause of death in Sade's fictions. It is in *Juliette*, however, that the libertines' ambivalent attitude to fire is most apparent. Here, volcanic fire is an object of their awe but also a rival to be bested. The heroine is excited at

Pietra-Mala by the volcano's all-consuming flames and aspires to emulate nature's destructiveness. From being a mere pupil of libertinism as she gazes on Pietra-Mala, by the time she reaches Vesuvius she is a libertine master, capable of the very worst excesses, and of a mind not merely to imitate nature, but to join her libertine friend Clairwil in defying her. Tiring of their companion, Olympe Borghèse, Juliette and Clairwil decide to cast her into the bowels of Vesuvius, for the sexual thrill the murder will afford them, but also as a direct challenge to nature: 'if what we have done is a true outrage to Nature, then let her avenge herself, for she can if she wishes; let an eruption occur, let lava boil up from that inferno down there, let a cataclysm snuff out our lives this very instant . . .' (*Juliette*). Juliette triumphantly celebrates their victory over nature's apparent impotence: 'Through our deed we were insulting Nature, defying her, baiting her; and triumphant in the impunity in which her unconcern left us, we looked to be profiting from her indulgence only in order to irritate her the more grievously'.

The volcanic cremation of Olympe and the burning of Marianne mark the culmination of what libertinism makes possible, and what the libertine version of Enlightenment thinking sets out to justify: the subordination of all ethical and moral concerns to individual freedom, especially where the passions are concerned. And here, more than in any other scene of horror in Sade's 'libertine' fictions, we are confronted with the question that goes to the very heart of the moral dilemma that Sade's libertine writing poses: is the text presenting libertinism for the reader to admire or abhor?

In writings published under his own name, Sade claims that an outright condemnation of libertinism is his only intention. Libertinism must be shown as it really is if the reader is to be dissuaded from admiring it or, worse, taking it up. But all such statements by the author can easily be seen as hypocritical attempts to avoid censorship and justify the spicing up of stories for the purposes of making money. Critics are divided on this crucial issue and there is ample textual and other evidence to support either point of view. In fact, the author was probably motivated by a number of different, and perhaps contradictory, impulses. We know from his personal correspondence that Sade wrote *Justine* and *Juliette* partly to generate much-needed funds, and that he himself was perfectly aware of their controversial nature. However, in the end, we can judge the question from our reading of the text alone. Readers must decide for themselves whether this text suggests sexual fascination with the libertine as fantasy figure of unlimited power, or loathing for the abuse of that power on the part of an embittered victim of the *ancien régime* (the libertines are all wealthy and powerful figures in the institutions of pre-revolutionary France). Do they represent the tyrannical powers that imprisoned him, or are they the advocates of a personal freedom he craves? As so often in Sade, there are no easy answers.

$$7$$

VICTIMS

Justine is the Sadeian victim *par excellence*, but her victimhood is more complex than one might at first think. It is not Justine's virtue that makes life difficult for her – she finds ways of justifying to herself her acquiescence in the various sexual acts demanded of her – but the 'double-bind' situations that so frequently confront her. In these situations, which involve the choice between two evils, Justine shows herself to be as much a pragmatist as a *dévote* (religious prude). One of the best examples of the 'double-bind' is the episode at d'Esterval's 'cut-throat' inn in *The New Justine*, where travellers are routinely robbed and murdered. When Justine discovers d'Esterval's crimes, he challenges her to help the victims to escape; if she succeeds, she too will be set free, but if she fails, she will remain to witness the deaths of more unfortunates. The problem is gleefully posed by d'Esterval himself:

> 'I want the travellers who perish by my hands to be forewarned of my plans; I take pleasure in the knowledge that they are convinced they are in the house of a scoundrel; I want them to defend themselves; in a word, I aspire to defeat them by force. This circumstance excites me, inflames my senses; in a word, it is this that makes me get hard,

to the point where I absolutely must fuck somebody, whatever their age or sex. This is the role that I intend you to play, my angel, it is you who will attempt the impossible in all good faith to enable the victims to escape, or to urge them to defend themselves. If you manage to save a single one, you may escape with them. I promise you that I will not pursue you. But if the person succumbs, you will stay; and as you are virtuous, you will see that I am not wrong when I say that you will want to stay with all your heart, for you will be forever kept here by the hope of rescuing one of these unfortunates from my rage. If you escaped from my house, you would take with you the certain know-ledge that I would continue my activities and with it the mortal regret that you had not tried to save those who succumbed after your depar-ture; you would never forgive yourself for having missed an opportunity to perform this excellent deed; and, as I say, the hope of one day succeeding is sure to keep you captive for the rest of your life. You're going to tell me that all of this is pointless, and that when there are not so many precautions, you will slip away as soon as you can to lodge a complaint and denounce me. I would be a fool, indeed, my dear, if I had no response to this objection . . . if I did not destroy it victoriously with a single word. Listen to me, Justine, there is not a single day when I do not kill. It will take you six days to reach the nearest magistrates. That's six victims that you would have allowed to perish while trying to have me arrested. This is an impos-sible hypothesis (because I would flee the moment you were missing from the house), still that's six victims sacrificed for the most ridicu-lous of reasons.'

'I would be the cause of their destruction?'

'Yes, since you could have saved one of these victims by warning him, and in saving him, you could have saved the others. Well, Justine, was I wrong to say that I would keep you prisoner by convic-tion? Now, flee if you dare . . . flee, I tell you, the doors are all open!'

'Monsieur, said Justine dejected, your wickedness puts me in an impossible position!'

La Nouvelle Justine, my translation

Such situations – and there are many of them in Sade's fic-tion – present the victim with an acute moral dilemma. If Justine tries to prevent one evil, her actions result in a far greater one. It is, Justine herself concedes later, her very virtue that invites her to commit criminal acts.

Sade here raises an important ethical issue which could scarcely have been more topical at the time of writing in the revolutionary years: how can one justify the evil consequences of actions that proclaim themselves to be virtuous? This very question is directly relevant to a revolution which seeks to establish an ethical state on the basis of an unethical act, the act of regicide, which is repeated in the guillotining of thousands of aristocrats, the attempted erasure of potential future monarchs as much as the punishment and removal of accomplices of the *ancien régime*.

In such extreme circumstances, good and evil, virtue and vice may become virtually undecidable. Geoffrey Bennington usefully relates the Sadeian double-bind to Kant's view of the fundamental illegitimacy of all revolution. Every state, Kant says, is defined by a supreme legislative authority which must be sovereign, a sovereignty represented by a head of state. Given that legitimacy, it is contradictory to try to write the legitimacy of resistance into any constitution. Bennington quotes Kant: 'There can . . . be no rightful resistance on the part of the people to the legislative head of state . . .'[17] This is another double-bind. Like Justine, the people are thus complicit with abuse out of morality.

As Bennington points out, what Sade helps us to see in Kant is how the 'optimistic' view of the Enlightenment and the Revolution to which its ideas led is actually reliant on a moment of absolute perversion, the murder of the King. In the 'd'Esterval' passage and other 'double-bind' scenarios in his fiction, Sade forces his contemporaries to confront the unpalatable notion that the urge to do good can necessitate evil actions, reminding them that in the recent political upheaval, the new republic had derived its authority from a single illegitimate and horrific act, the beheading of the monarch.[18] Indeed, the entire *Justine* project is designed to show how an uncompromising devotion to virtue such as Robespierre's may easily have dire and bloody consequences.

The problem of good and evil is one that repeatedly confronts Justine, and it raises the question of how an all-powerful and benevolent deity could permit evil to come out of good, a problem that had defeated Voltaire earlier in the century, as Sade well knew. Voltaire's solution was to view the deity as a sort of indifferent clockmaker who, after winding the universe up like a clock, left it to run down on its own. Voltaire's deity, in other words, is very much an absent deity, much like the absent causes of existence in the universe for Sade.

The double-bind situations which confront Justine also demonstrate that the trials to which those one might call the 'chief' victims in Sade's world are subjected are not just physical but also – and perhaps more crucially – moral and psychological.

Victimhood is not just a passive state in Sade: the victim is frequently joined in debate by her libertine captors, her virtue (and arguments in its defence) tested to breaking-point. Like Justine, many victims are required to wrestle with libertine logic, and forced to respond to the theories put to them. The libertines derive as much satisfaction from defeating their victims intellectually as they do from subduing and abusing them physically, while the victims themselves (and Justine offers the best example of this) rise admirably to the challenge with equally forceful and reasoned replies. (The resilient and often feisty Justine does this immediately following this extract.)

It is as if Sade were constantly drawn to dialogue with the victim that he himself had become, to interrogate the reasons for his own victimhood through Justine, to put the victim's side of his own nature to the test of logical reasoning and debate. Like her, he would prefer to choose virtue, but like her he is confronted with the problem that virtuous actions can have evil consequences. From the victim's point of view, it is more dangerous to have a girl kept in ignorance of vice than to educate her in the ways of the world. By the same token, the ostensibly well-intentioned attempts to protect society by imprisoning wrong-doers like the author only serve to turn them into hardened recidivists who will then become an even greater threat to others on their release.

What the above passage illustrates above all is that acts of violence in Sade always have a philosophical underpinning and a philosophical context. Such acts are not presented for their own sake, as they would be in some modern forms of violent pornography, for example, but as exemplifications of a philosophical point, or as a pretext for philosophical debate. These passages also together constitute an important body of evidence for viewing Sade as a moralist.

Note the self-conscious irony of Justine's later observation, 'How discouraging the story of my life will be for all souls if ever it is published!' Sade's moral position is a deeply pessimistic one, formed by his own experiences in the prisons of both the *ancien régime* and the Terror, but the caustic irony of lines like this which pepper the writing reveals an enduring ability to mock his own misfortune. Although Justine herself is never allowed to do this, we can just make out in the shadows of the narrative an empathizing author-figure, winking knowingly at the reader: 'You will find this tale disheartening,' he seems to be saying, 'but only if you take it too seriously!'

★

Juliette has finished her long story, told to her sister, Justine, and a handful of male libertines. Juliette and her unscrupulous companions have become tired of their pious friend (Juliette refuses to keep such a prude in the house) and determine to be rid of her. Justine must of course perish eventually, since uncompromising virtue must be shown to fail as a game-plan in a society driven by vice. In the first two versions of *Justine*, nature alone bears responsibility for her death when the unfortunate young woman is accidentally struck by a thunderbolt in a raging storm, while in the final version of her death, in *Juliette*, the libertines drive her outside, entrusting her fate to the elements and nature. Responsibility for Justine's demise is, therefore, shared between nature and her wicked companions:

> Lightning glitters, the wind howls, the clouds boil as though in a caldron, all the firmament is seething. One might have said that nature, tired of her works, was readying to confound all her elements in order to force them to adopt new forms. Justine is shown the door; not only is she not given as much as a penny, she is sent forth stripped of the little that remained to her. Bewildered, humiliated by such ingratitude and so many abominations, but too content to escape what could have been worse still, the child of woe, murmuring thanks to God, totters past the chateau gates and down the lane leading to the highroad ... Scarcely does she reach it when a flash of lightning breaks from the heavens, and she is struck down, smitten by a thunderbolt that pierces her through.
>
> 'She is dead!' cry the villains, clapping their hands and hastening to where Justine lies upon the ground. 'Come quickly, Madame, come contemplate heaven's handiwork, come see how the powers above reward piety and goodness. Love virtue, we are told, and behold the fate reserved for its most devoted servitors.'
>
> Our four libertines surround the corpse; and although it has been horribly disfigured, frightful designs nevertheless shape themselves in libertine minds, the shattered vestiges of the defunct Justine become the object of lewd covetings. The infamous Juliette excites her friends as they snatch the clothes from the body. The lightning, entering by way of the mouth, had burst out through the vagina; fierce jests are made upon the path by which the fire of heaven chose to visit the victim.
>
> 'Yes,' Noirceuil said, 'praise be to God, he merits it; there you

have the proof of his decency: he left the ass untouched. It is still a
beautiful thing, this sublime behind which caused so much fuck to
flow; does it not tempt you, Chabert?'

And by way of reply the mischievous Abbé inserts his prick to the
height of the balls in that lifeless hulk. His example is shortly followed by the others; unto her ashes they all four insult that dear girl,
one by one; the execrable Juliette, watching them, frigs herself without pause; and finally the company retires, abandoning the corpse by
the wayside. Woeful and ill-starred creature, 'twas written on high
that not even the repose of death would safeguard you from the
atrocities of crime and the perversity of mankind.

Juliette

It is hard to be sympathetic with the wretched Justine in this
final scene of her tragic life. The 'bewildered' and 'humiliated'
heroine has clearly learnt nothing from the many abuses committed against her by a succession of unscrupulous libertines.
On the other hand, the death of Justine may be read as symbolic, not real, an event rich in metaphorical meanings.

The real focus of this dénouement to the long
Justine/Juliette saga is not Justine's death but the libertines'
defiant challenge to nature, here, as so often elsewhere in
Sade, a substitute for the non-existent divinity. Noirceuil will,
he has declared, 'embrace the true faith if the elements spare
her'.

The image of nature presented here is far removed from
Rousseau's idealized view of an earthly utopia, inhabited by
noble savages and uncorrupted by the evils of civilization.
The violence of the storm exemplifies the savagery of nature
while the 'perversity of mankind' as displayed here by
Noirceuil, Juliette and the rest is a grotesque parody of
Rousseau's belief in man's natural goodness. Sadeian nature,
however, is not merely dispassionate, neutral in its treatment of
human beings, for, as in Voltaire's *Candide*, it seems to single
out the virtuous for its harshest blows. Justine's death rams

home the central and oft-repeated message in Sade that virtue just does not pay. Nature, which Justine had thought essentially good, is the very agent of her destruction, whether in the shape of the storm that kills her or of the wickedness of the human beings around her.

The cleaving asunder of Justine's body by a thunderbolt that enters her mouth and exits through her vagina is, for Angela Carter, a parody of the very act of birth. We might also be tempted to see it as a symbolic reversal of that event, as the vagina becomes the channel for the destruction, not the creation of life. If Sadeian Man cannot forgive nature for giving birth to him, for plunging him into a godless and hostile universe, or woman for acting as nature's accomplice, then what more fitting end for the quasi-maternal Justine, everywoman's representative, as the site of man's symbolic unbirth. This symbolic act is literalized earlier in *Juliette*, when Borchamps forces a daughter, Ernelinde, to cut open her mother's womb:

> 'You received your existence here,' says the cruel father once the opening has been made, 'you must now return into the womb whence you emerged.'
>
> She is garrotted, then pressed, twisted until by dint of much force and considerable art, there she is, breathing still, back inside the loins that once gave her to the world.
>
> *Juliette*

The heavy irony of nature's sparing Justine's posterior is not simply a reminder of the libertines' penchant for sodomy, but a symbolic linking of the sublime and the abject, of the divine and the debased. (The posterior is indeed the only part of the female body which the libertines are wont to describe as 'divine'.)

Mikhail Bakhtin's theories of the carnivalesque in literature may be of some use here. Bakhtin has shown that carnival is above all an *inversion*. The reversal in this scene of the poles of the physical body (the face and the posterior), so that the latter replaces the former as the traditional site and expression of female beauty, is characteristic of the Bakhtinian theory of carnival. In this Bakhtinian perspective, the storm scenario itself can be read as a carnivalesque inversion, as the heavens hurl thunder to the earth, and the earthiest part of Justine's body is deified by the libertines. The carnival is a fundamentally hedonistic event, and the company certainly derive pleasure from Justine's death, both sadistic and erotic. But as the single day in the year when servant becomes master and peasant becomes monarch, the carnival is also an implicitly violent event, in that it enjoins us to overturn hierarchies, and to perform transgressive acts that would normally be considered taboo. The Sadeian erotic always springs from transgression, and, in this further respect, is strongly carnivalesque.[19]

The eroticism here is focused on necrophilia, defined as an erotic attraction to corpses, one of the most transgressive acts conceivable. This perversion is extremely rare in reality, but a number of Sade's libertines in *Juliette* do engage in activities that appear necrophilic in character, although, as here, the eroticism seems to derive from the transgressive and fetishistic nature of the act rather than from a specific focus on the dead body as a sexually arousing object. The abbess Delbène, for example, has herself fucked on the corpses of her victims, while Juliette's and Durand's using the bones of their victims as dildos is a particularly macabre example of surreal humour. Cordelli, exceptionally, appears to derive pleasure from the very action of fucking and sodomizing the corpse of his own daughter, whom he has himself poisoned. But even here, the knowledge of his multiple transgressions – in addition to necrophilia, he commits murder, incest, sodomy and blasphemy (the event takes place in church) – framed by the voyeurism of Juliette and Durand who are watching secretly, seems to overshadow the necrophilic act itself. At the same time, necrophilia is a graphic expression of the libertine's megalomania, in that the dead body's utter defencelessness allows him to enact the fantasy of total domination.

Like so many Sadeian victims before her in the *Justine/Juliette* saga, Justine is finally fragmented into her sexual parts, frozen permanently as the fleshy sex-toy she has fought throughout her short life to avoid becoming. If the Sadeian woman cannot manage to be a female counterpart of her male libertine companions (like the priapic and amoral Juliette), then she is doomed eventually to die. The reduction to the sexual function, devoid of all humanity, often precedes the death of the victim, but death allows and sometimes, as here, effects a physical dismemberment that grotesquely parodies this reductionism. Like those rubber replicas of the female sexual parts sold in modern sex-shops, Justine is now no more than an orifice – in this case, an anal one. Of course, this literal reification can happen to men, too. Earlier in the novel, the man-hating Clairwil cuts off and embalms a monk's penis for use as a dildo.

This fragmentation of the human body can be a subject for serious art as well as inspiration for the pornographic wares of the sex industry. In his controversial images of dolls, for example, the surrealist artist Hans Bellmer represents the female's (and sometimes the female child's) body in terms of its sexual organs. Such images perhaps remind us that we are all at times objectified and fragmented, physically and sexually, but also psychologically, victims of the defining and eroticizing gaze of others.

These extracts highlight the female victim's dual role in Sade's libertine writings: a sexual cipher and a stereotype of feminine beauty, certainly, but also an opponent to be defeated in moral and philosophical debate. The victim's complex function mirrors the libertine's own complexity. Driven by sexual desires of a fetishistic and sadistic nature focused obsessively on the bodies of angelic young females, the male libertine does not actually enjoy the total freedom from moral doubt that he demands of others (see Chapter 6). If he did so, he would not feel obliged to dialogue with his victim, to defeat her intellectually as well as physically, to convince her (and himself) that his actions are philosophically justified. As in the master–slave relationship identified by Hegel, libertines and victims are thus locked together by a mutual dependency that may well have its origins in the author's own unconscious needs.

8

THE AMBIVALENT FEMININE

On the night of 16 February 1779, in his prison cell in the fortress of Vincennes, Sade had a vivid dream. He had fallen asleep reading a biography of the fourteenth-century poet Petrarch, which his uncle, the abbé de Sade, had recently published to much critical acclaim. It was a freezing cold night in the middle of winter and Sade had been reading the book to comfort himself before closing his eyes.

Petrarch had dedicated many poems to a beautiful young woman named Laura, whom Sade's uncle identified as a family ancestor, Laure de Noves, wife of Hugues de Sade. This is how Donatien described the dream in a letter to his wife the following day:

> It was around midnight. I had just fallen asleep, his Memoires in my hand. All of a sudden, she appeared to me . . . I saw her! The horror of the tomb had not impaired the splendour of her beauty and her eyes had the same fire as when Petrarch sang of them. She was completely swathed in black mourning crepe, over which spilled her lovely blonde hair. It seemed as if love, in order to make her more beautiful, sought to soften the lugubrious array in which she offered herself to my gaze. 'Why dost thou groan on earth?' she asked me. 'Come join me. No more sufferings, no more wars, no more sorrow, no

more trouble in the endless space where I dwell. Have the courage to follow me there.' Hearing which, I threw myself at her feet and said to her: 'Oh, my Mother! . . .' And sobs stifled my voice. She held out a hand to me, which I covered with my tears, and she wept too. 'I took pleasure in seeing into the future,' she added, 'when I lived in this world that you detest. I looked at each generation succeeding me until I came to you, and did not imagine you so unhappy.' Then, overcome by my affection and despair, I flung my arms around her neck to hold on to her or follow her, and to bathe her in my tears, but the ghost vanished, and I was left alone with my sorrow.

My translation

There has in the past been a tendency on the part of some of the more prominent female critics of Sade to view the Sadeian woman as a positive, even heroic, figure. Juliette, declares Angela Carter, 'fucks at least as much as she is fucked'.[20] Sade, Carter claims, is 'obviously not for women or against women', he is 'unencumbered by prejudice against women'.[21] Yet attitudes to women expressed in Sade's writings, both fiction and non-fiction, are fraught with ambivalence. In the anonymous novels, the simple duality of virgin and whore, of female victim and female libertine, as represented by the two sisters, Justine and Juliette, is probably the most striking manifestation of this ambivalence. But the apparent simplicity of this division of women into two stereotyped categories is misleading, concealing a complex set of unconscious psychological and sexual attitudes. From a psychological point of view, such attitudes do appear to shift constantly between the two extremes of love and hate, a movement that expresses itself sexually in terms of excessive desire on the one hand and excessive disgust on the other. We saw in Chapter 6 how female libertines in Sade's fictions are recuperated into a masculine world, neutralizing problems associated with their femininity.

Some critics have suggested that the more negative attitudes towards the feminine may have their origins in Donatien's early experiences. The maternal neglect that was a feature of his childhood would help to explain a certain antipathy to mothers, while a succession of unhappy love affairs may have engendered a deep-rooted cynicism in the sensitive adolescent, the beginnings of a tendency to resent the power of feminine beauty. Wearing his heart on his sleeve far too often, and profoundly wounded by rejection, the young Marquis may well have erected emotional barriers against future hurt, seeking refuge in sexual indulgence as an antidote to the vicissitudes of romantic love. This emotional and psychological ambivalence may have helped to shape Sade's early sexual proclivities. Although Sade himself never openly confessed to practising sodomy, there is some evidence that he did so with his valet on a number of occasions, and in the anonymous fictions, many of the libertines express a marked preference for the male body, even those who are sometimes willing to have sex with women.

Yet it is undeniable that women did occupy an important place in Sade's affections, and Sade's own correspondence certainly expresses attitudes and ideas which directly conflict with the views of his libertine characters, and the perception of women which emerges from the biographical evidence available appears to be at odds with the hypothesis of a wholly negative representation of the feminine and even of the maternal in his works. The reader of this correspondence addressed mostly to his wife, Renée-Pélagie, during the Marquis's long period of detention in the 1770s and 1780s, will come across genuine expressions of love for a number of women, including his grandmother, close friend of the Sade family Milli Rousset and, above all, Renée-Pélagie herself.

When one reads the letters Sade wrote to his wife over

thirteen years, one cannot help but be struck by the sincerity of his affection for her. Yet during the long years of his imprisonment, Renée-Pélagie's letters and visits provide the only source of comfort for him, and there are times when the tone of his letters to her suggests that he perceives her as fulfilling a maternal rather than a wifely role, as he begs her to procure for him a particular kind of cake or throws a temper tantrum when she fails to bring him chocolate.

But other mother-substitutes occasionally haunt the Marquis's correspondence. One particular letter, an extract from which began this chapter, reveals a passionate and deep-seated devotion to a maternal figure from the distant past. This remarkable letter tells us much about Sade's state of mind at this time, but it also suggests personality traits that help us to understand the profound motivations behind both his fictional work and his philosophical and political writings. The vision is certainly steeped in self-pity, and there is a barely concealed rage against his misfortune. On the other hand, Sade represents himself here as an emotional and sensitive figure, suffering above all from loneliness and a sense of abandonment. Nevertheless, in spite of any attempt on Sade's part to manipulate the reader, it is still possible to discern a strong romantic sensibility in these lines which may surprise those for whom the Marquis's name is synonymous only with perversion and pornography.

Laura is represented in Sade's dream as unchanged in beauty, her body uncorrupted, and in this sense may be interpreted as the expression in Sade's unconscious of a quest for perfection beyond the grave. From a psychoanalytic point of view, these visions of a body whose physical perfection has survived the ravages of death are the invention of a psychotic or narcissistic personality as a protection against the threat of physical disintegration – a characteristic of a megalomania that refuses to die.

Perfection or superlativity is a universal characteristic of physical descriptions of women in Sade's fictions, where it fulfils a variety of functions. In addition to the evocation of a perfect or ideal female body ('the most beautiful arse I had ever seen!'), the superlative cliché may also have a polarizing effect, reducing ideals of beauty, but also of good and evil, to a banal shorthand. At the same time, this banality seems to mock the idealized image of female perfection it conveys. In *The New Justine*, when the bandit Cœur-de-Fer has violently ripped Justine's clothing from her body with his knife, creating a perfect opportunity for voyeuristic detail, the lascivious reader must instead be content with vague suggestiveness: 'In an instant the most beautiful body in the world was exposed for a second time to the most monstrous manifestations of lewdness.' Such polarizations strain credulity, taking the reader into a fairy-tale world in which beauty and ugliness, good and evil are facile and simplistic concepts, in which the feminine is idealized and in the end made unreal.

The bubble of unreality bursts when the woman becomes a mother. Motherhood, the most graphic expression of nature, makes the lovely girl an irascible and ugly witch. Mothers in Sade's fiction are almost always negative figures that bar access to their young and nubile daughters. Worst of all, mothers always let you down. Sade expresses here a yearning for a mother-figure impossible to grasp. Indeed, Laura represents the ideal mother that Sade never had. His mother, the Comtesse, appeared to take very little interest in her only child, and her relative absence from his childhood is often seen as the possible source of the mother-hatred that permeates Sade's adult writings.

When he wrote the 'Laura' letter, Sade was thirty-eight years old and he had been in prison for the best part of two years. His mental state obviously suffered from his long periods of solitary confinement. His paranoid tendencies were heightened to the extent that he became convinced that Madame de Montreuil, his mother-in-law, was waging a campaign against him and was single-handedly responsible for his plight. Relations that had previously basked in mutual admiration were now irretrievably embittered. It is reasonable to conjecture that the mother-figures of the fiction may be unconsciously influenced by the Présidente as much as by the author's own mother. Like Madame de Montreuil, mothers in Sade wish to prevent licentious behaviour, especially with their young daughters (Sade had angered his mother-in-law by seducing her youngest daughter, Anne-Prospère). Eventually haunting Sade's letters week by week as a loathsome creature vomited from hell and a vampire sucking his blood and that of his children, Madame de Montreuil ends up as a kind of prototype for the maternal victims of his fictions, the principal focus of his venom and hatred. At the same time, there are self-consciously ironic, if not blackly humorous, undertones in much of this anti-Montreuil rhetoric. Like some modern stand-up comic telling tasteless mother-in-law jokes, Sade inveighs against the Présidente with a regularity and a hyperbole that is theatrical, as in these smouldering lines written in February 1783: 'This morning, in the midst of my own suffering, I saw her, the bitch, being flayed alive, dragged upon a heap of burning coals and then thrown into a vat of vinegar.'

We noted earlier that the ambivalence towards the feminine expresses itself sexually in terms of both an extreme attraction and an equally extreme repulsion. The female body is a universal object of obsessive desire in Sade's fiction, and yet it can provoke equally strong feelings of hostility and disgust. Indeed, the overwhelming majority of Sade's female characters are consistently represented as objects: objects of desire, and yet of simultaneous contempt ('I get pleasure from women, but I despise them; more than that, I detest them as soon as my passion is sated,' says Jérôme in *The New Justine*); objects of exchange (they marry each other's daughters, or, like Jérôme and his cousin, give each other their sisters) and, especially, objects of violence and even consumption. The breasts and the vagina of their female victims are repeatedly bitten, pricked, whipped and stabbed. Sade's libertines frequently declare their aversion for the female genitals, which they insist be kept hidden from view.

What Jérôme and others like him hate about the female body is a kind of absence, one that is manifestly physical. Absence is equally characteristic of nature itself, which the libertine also hates because it works in an apparently motiveless and arbitrary fashion. For Sadeian Man, nature and the female body are one, and for the same reasons are objects of fascination and repulsion. The female body bleeds every month, and serves nature's reproductive aims. The female body is also a negative, rather than a positive, female genitals an absence not a presence. This physical absence is an obscenity for Sade's male libertine – 'the horror of that which cannot be seen in woman' in Luce Irigaray's expression – because it figures a lack that is impossible to master, a lack for which nature is to blame: 'That's what a woman is, then!' cries the young Jérôme at the first sight of his naked sister, '[. . .] oh! what's beautiful about that! [. . .] what extraordinary contrariness has led nature not to enrich with all its graces that part of the woman's body that makes her different from us? For there's no doubt that that's what men seek out; and *what's desirable about a place where there is nothing*?' (*La Nouvelle Justine*, my translation and my emphasis.)

Nature, then, is responsible for female absence, which itself inescapably becomes a metonym for nature's absent causes. The female body is the sign and symbol of nature's disappointing nullity, while nature is a lover and a mother who, like the spectral vision of the dream, is never *really* there. The Laura of Sade's dream is the idealized image of the maternal (Sade calls her his mother) and the sexual (he dwells on her physical beauty), but like all dream images, she eventually vanishes, leaving the prisoner alone with his sorrow. In the profoundest of senses, ambivalent attitudes both to Laura and to all the other women of Sade's fictions are an unconscious expression of the anguish of solitary Man, abandoned in an empty universe.

9

SEX ON THE STAGE

Philosophy in the Boudoir, a virtually unperformable piece of live theatre outside any pornographic context, exemplifies the physical potential of drama taken to its ultimate logical extreme. Sade brilliantly exploits this potential to demonstrate the interdependence of the intellect and the body, and the dangers of a political culture that denies both the power of sex and its synergy with violence. Published anonymously in 1795, after Sade's repeated failure to establish himself as a conventional playwright, the work also displays a physical and verbal black humour that works better on Sade's virtual stage than it ever would have done in the Paris theatres.

In this extract, Eugénie's hapless mother falls victim to her own daughter, having arrived to rescue her from the libertines who are giving her lessons in the theory and the practice of sex. Assisted by her libertine mentors, who rape and bugger Madame de Mistival before infecting her with the pox, Eugénie enthusiastically agrees to sew up her mother's vagina and anus to prevent the disease from escaping and to hasten its deleterious effects.

MADAME DE SAINT-ANGE: I believe it is now of the highest importance to provide against the escape of the poison circulating in Madame's veins; consequently, Eugénie must very carefully sew your cunt and ass so that the virulent humor, more concentrated, less subject to evaporation and not at all to leakage, will more promptly cinder your bones.

EUGÉNIE: Excellent idea! Quickly, quickly, fetch me needle and thread! . . . Spread your thighs, Mamma, so I can stitch you together – so that you'll give me no more little brothers and sisters. (MADAME DE SAINT-ANGE *gives* EUGÉNIE *a large needle, through whose eye is threaded a heavy red waxed thread;* EUGÉNIE *sews.*)

[. . .]

MADAME DE MISTIVAL: You are tearing me to pieces, vile creature! . . . Oh, how I blush that it was I who gave you life!

EUGÉNIE: Come, come, be quiet, Mother dear; it's finished.

DOLMANCÉ, *emerging, with a great erection, from* MADAME DE SAINT-ANGE*'s hands*: Eugénie, allow me to do the ass; that part belongs to me.

MADAME DE SAINT-ANGE: You're too stiff, Dolmancé, you'll make a martyr of her.

DOLMANCÉ: What matter! have we not written permission to make of her what we please? (*He turns* MADAME DE MISTIVAL *upon her stomach, catches up the needle, and begins to sew her asshole.*)

MADAME DE MISTIVAL, *screaming like a banshee*: Aïe! aïe! aïe!

DOLMANCÉ, *driving the needle deep into her flesh*: Silence, bitch! or I'll make a hash of your buttocks . . . Eugénie, frig me . . .

EUGÉNIE: Willingly, but upon condition you prick her more energetically, for, you must admit, you are proceeding with strange forbearance. (*She frigs him.*)

[. . .]

MADAME DE MISTIVAL: Oh pardon me, Monsieur, I beg your pardon a thousand thousand times over . . . you are killing me . . .

DOLMANCÉ, *wild with pleasure*: I should like to . . . 'tis an age since I have had such an erection; never would I have thought it possible after so many consecutive ejaculations.

[. . .]

DOLMANCÉ, *who has finished his task, does nothing but increase his stabbing of the victim's buttocks as he discharges*: Ah triple

bloody fucking God! . . . my sperm flows . . . 'tis lost, by bleed-
ing little Jesus! . . . Eugénie, direct it upon the flanks I have just
mutilated . . . oh fuck! fuck! 'tis done . . . over . . . I've no
more . . . oh, why must weakness succeed passions so alive? . . .

MADAME DE SAINT-ANGE: Fuck! fuck me, brother, I discharge! . . .
(*To* AUGUSTIN): Stir yourself, great fucking-john! Don't you know
that it is when I come that you've got to sink your tool deepest
into my ass? . . . Ah, sacred name of God! how sweet it is, thus
to be fucked by two men . . . (*The group disperses.*)

DOLMANCÉ: And now all's been said. (*To* MADAME DE MISTIVAL):
Hey! whore, you may clothe yourself and leave when you wish. I
must tell you that your husband authorized the doing of all that
has just been done to you. We told you as much; you did not
believe it. (*He shows her the letter.*) May this example serve to
remind you that your daughter is old enough to do what she
pleases; that she likes to fuck, loves to fuck, that she was born
to fuck, and that, if you do not wish to be fucked yourself, the
best thing for you to do is to let her do what she wants. Get out;
the Chevalier will escort you home. [. . .] (*After the Chevalier's
departure and* MADAME DE MISTIVAL*'s*): And now, good friends,
let's to dinner, and afterward the four of us will retire for the
night . . . in the same bed. Well, we've had a fine active day. I
never dine so heartily, I never sleep so soundly as when I have,
during the day, sufficiently befouled myself with what our fools
call crimes.

Philosophy in the Bedroom

Sade valued his theatrical output above all else but he in fact
achieved little success in getting his plays performed. The
themes of his formally conventional dramas are recognizably
Sadeian – seduction, betrayal, incest, the vicissitudes of fate –
but the dramatic scenarios and passages of certain of his libertine works (*Philosophy in the Boudoir, Juliette, Dialogue between
a Priest and a Dying Man*, for example) are more interestingly
innovative and less self-consciously designed to impress as
serious grand theatre.

This memorable spectacle from *Philosophy in the Boudoir*

reads like a piece of modern-day 'theatre of the absurd'. On one level, the scene contains verbal humour and physical comedy that transform its tragic potential into black farce. The very notion of germs 'falling out' of the mother's vagina if the hole is not properly sewn up may not be foreign to a rudimentary eighteenth-century medical science, but it is absurdly comic to the modern reader. This detail, together with other farcical aspects, makes it hard to read the scene on a realistic level. Eugénie's actions imply a fantastic use of the mother as object that is funny, in part precisely *because* it is so unthinkable. The transformation of living creatures into things for the purposes of visual humour is a notable characteristic of certain modern cartoons, which depict an extreme though sanitized violence, from which the victim always recovers (*Tom and Jerry* springs immediately to mind, but also its postmodern pastiche, the far more violent *Itchy & Scratchy* watched by the Simpsons). The farcical comedy of Sade's 'needlework' scene operates in essentially the same fashion.

Does the mother secretly enjoy her appalling treatment? If, as some critics have suggested, Sade the author is far less a sadist than a masochist who in some ways identifies with his female victims (in particular, with Justine), this unthinkable idea cannot be rejected out of hand. After all, the curiously low-key nature of her verbal responses to the pain inflicted upon her is at once comically inappropriate and suggestively ambivalent: 'Oh pardon me, Monsieur, I beg your pardon a thousand thousand times over . . .' might almost be read as the stylized language of the masochist, engaged in a theatre of violence and pain that is in fact consensual. Looked at in this way, the possibility of experiencing a masochistic thrill as the helpless sexualized victim of a group of young, healthy and attractive individuals is not entirely implausible. Indeed, many current SM practices resemble the 'closing-up' of Madame de

Mistival: from rubber suits to genital restraints, contemporary masochists derive intense sexual pleasure from the total domination and control of their bodies by others.

Whether sadist or masochist, no one, in fact, involved in this scenario can be described as a sexual innocent. Even the apprentice seamstress Eugénie is no longer the blushing young virgin by the time her mother arrives to rescue her from the clutches of the libertines. She not only asserts her authority with surprising firmness – she commands Dolmancé to masturbate her and peremptorily chides the Chevalier for his outspokenness – she takes control of the entire proceedings, performing the principal role with gusto and directing the others to fulfil their parts as she sees fit. A play within a play, the 'needlework' scene is self-conscious knockabout theatre, an especially cruel 'Punch and Judy' show, in which Judy proves even more vicious than Punch (Eugénie's 'you are proceeding with strange forbearance' to Dolmancé suggests the familiar Sadeian notion that women have the potential to be more cruel than men); a sinister comic melodrama, directed by and starring the ingénue herself.

The comedy follows a long tradition of pure farce stretching back to *commedia dell'arte*, Chaucer and Boccaccio, such that the visual humour of the tableau overrides any erotic potential. There is the physical 'daisy-chain' of characters linked together by sexual penetration, a thread running from pain to pleasure and echoed in the ambiguous and exaggerated cries of all actors in the scenario. Madame de Mistival's 'you are killing me' is actually a mistranslation of the original French, 'vous me faîtes mourir! . . .' ('you're making me die! . . .') which closely resembles the libertines' own favourite exclamation of pleasure at the moment of orgasm. Indeed, the suspension marks of the original text invite the reader to supply the missing term.

Thus, the scene's visual comedy subtly merges with a verbal humour to be found earlier on. Commenting upon what she had learnt in a single day, as she had prepared to fuck her mother with a dildo, Eugénie had made the kind of statement favoured by Sade's libertines who rejoice in the condensation of a number of perversities in a single act. The statement was above all a piece of self-conscious irony, an exclamation of delight in the performance of a sexual act, that trangressed several taboos at once. The delight is as much linguistic as sexual, as suggested by the daughter's joyful listing of her crimes: 'EUGÉNIE: Come, dear lovely Mamma, come, let me serve you as a husband. 'Tis a little thicker than your spouse's, is it not, my dear? Never mind, 'twill enter . . . Ah, Mother dear, you cry, you scream, scream when your daughter fucks you! . . . And you, Dolmancé, you bugger me! . . . Here I am: at one stroke incestuous, adulteress, sodomite, and all that in a girl who only lost her maidenhead today! . . . What progress, my friends!'

The humour of the scene also includes the parody of dramatic conventions and social mores through their ironic inversion.

On an intertextual level, the arrival of the mother and her subsequent mistreatment is a clear parody of the recognition or reunion scenes common in the dénouements of the sentimental novel in the eighteenth century (Rousseau's *The New Héloise* offers well-known examples of this device). The dramatic convention of the *deus ex machina* that saves the day at the last moment in the comedies and melodramas of the seventeenth and eighteenth centuries (in the form of a King's messenger, for example, or a hero rescuing a young female victim) is wholly inverted here, as the mother-rescuer falls prey to the daughter she has come to save. The Shakespearean tones of the first line of Dolmancé's closing speech, addressed as much to the audience as to the other characters – 'And now all's been said and done' – suggest a parody of all those pieces of virtuous theatre in which the ending points the moral lesson, piously delivered by one of the leading protagonists. Dolmancé's brandishing of a letter which he claims is from Monsieur de Mistival and gives them permission to do whatever they like with his wife is reminiscent of royal letters and warrants presented in the dénouements of Molière plays to set the world to rights, a paternal hand of authority restoring order and quietening quarrelsome children, while reaffirming and underlining the Father/King's indivisible sovereignty. In this case, of course, the Father's Law brings disharmony not harmony, supporting rather than punishing crime, and undermining rather than reuniting the family. At the same time, we note that the father remains the sole source of power, dispensing rights as he alone sees fit. Wives and daughters are still the property of men, even in the libertine utopia constructed in Sade's text, in which females who dare to be libertines are alleged to enjoy as much freedom as men. The truth is that the masculine position is and remains the default position of authority and power.

The libertine society is not only a patriarchy, it also adheres rigidly to the old class structures, according to which working people have a use-value as servants or labourers or an exchange-value as commodities. In social gatherings of any kind, they are non-persons, invisible unless required to perform some task. This is precisely the manner in which Augustin, Saint-Ange's gardener, is treated. Sexually well-endowed and gifted with vigorous orgasms – we were told earlier that his member is thirteen inches long and eight and a half in circumference, and that he discharges like a waterfall – Augustin is nothing other than a walking penis: his only function is that of a living dildo. He himself knows that he is not

the equal of his masters and mistresses: when offered Eugénie
as a 'bed of flowers' ready for digging, he responded with the
deference that would have been expected of him as a mere
employee: 'Oh, Jemmy, Sir! Such neat little oddments ain't
made for such as me'. Mostly referred to in the third person,
Augustin is a spear-carrier (in more senses than one), not a
main player, and, as such, speaks only when spoken to. When
he is addressed directly, as he is here by Saint-Ange, it is always
in a rough or chiding manner. He is a 'ninny', a 'great pig',
'not fit for civilized society', an 'imbecile', and here a 'great
fucking-john' who is berated by his mistress for not pleasuring
her properly. He is dragged into the boudoir from the garden
where he rightly belongs, precisely because he is an extension
of the natural world, a living example of nature's privileging of
the pleasure-principle. However, when the discussion turned
to politics, religion and morality in a previous scene, Augustin
was sent back outside since these matters are not for his ears.
Sade's sexual utopia is a fundamentally élitist one, and ideas
that might have a dangerous influence on simple minds must
remain the preserve of a well-educated, paternalistic minority,
born and bred to lead the way.

There is parody of social manners and customs in the very
choice of needle and thread as the weapons of torture. Sewing
in eighteenth-century society was an activity typically reserved
for unmarried young women, unmarriageable spinsters and
long-married old matrons. Sewing, one might conjecture,
busies idle fingers that might otherwise find less wholesome
preoccupations. But in this parody of the sewing-circle, the
feminine creation (of cloths and tapestries) becomes the
destruction of the feminine in the form of Eugénie's mother.
Sade, moreover, explodes the sexist stereotype according to
which sewing is the unique preserve of women by passing the
needle to Dolmancé, just as the heterosexual norm of vaginal

sex is replaced by a preoccupation with the bisexual anus – the male libertine claims the right to sew up this particular part of Madame de Mistival's anatomy.

A mere substitute for sex in conventional society, sewing is, then, here, overtly sexualized. Like the dildo that Eugénie strapped on moments earlier to rape her mother, the needle-phallus penetrates the mother's body, but, inverting sexual and cultural norms associated with the penetration of women, the daughter's intention is both to prevent the creation of new life and to remove the potential for sexual pleasure.

In modern English vernacular, one might say that the mother is well and truly 'stitched up' by this gang of delinquents. Eugénie refers with distaste on more than one occasion to her mother's sexual activity (which is entirely limited to the marital chamber and, we assume, to procreation – for all Sadeian libertines, that most hated and despised of all sexual aims). Wearing a strap-on dildo, Eugénie has already served her mother 'as a husband', and in this passage, she is delighted to prevent her mother from giving her 'more little brothers and sisters'. Angela Carter has commented usefully on this anti-procreation motif with reference to Melanie Klein's theories of the 'good' and 'bad' breasts, arguing that Eugénie sews her mother up to avoid having to compete with any future siblings for maternal nourishment by the 'good breast', symbol of the satisfaction of basic human needs.[22] The Sadeian libertine unconsciously desires his enjoyment of the world to be undisturbed by the presence of others.

The crime for which the mother has been 'stitched up' or framed, then, is the crime she suspects her daughter of committing, that of sexual congress, for does not the sewing operation amount to the fitting of a literal and extreme form of chastity belt, or even to a form of female circumcision, both of which are designed to impede female sexual activity?

Eugénie's action does, of course, represent another ironic inversion of contemporary social norms, in that it is not the daughter's sexuality that must be curbed but the mother's. There is undeniably a sense in which the entire scene dramatizes, albeit in extreme form, the age-old war between parents and children, between the younger and older generations, a favourite theme of French comic theatre since Molière a century earlier. In this perspective, Dolmancé becomes the wild but sexy older man, the quite unsuitable boyfriend who might seduce the mother too, given half a chance. The closing up of the mother's sexual orifices deprives her of her ability to remain sexually active and so prevents her from competing sexually with the daughter, whose orifices have just been opened up. The needle scene is most transparently about the way in which the sexual availability of women depended in Sade's time upon the removal from their mothers of authority in sexual matters. In this sense, it is socially as well as morally transgressive.

Extending this reading to a biographical level, if we regard Dolmancé, the main protagonist, as a persona of the author, Madame de Mistival becomes, from his point of view, the classic 'mother-in-law' figure, embodied in the authorial imagination by the Présidente de Montreuil, mythical object of hatred and contempt to be symbolically punished for her spiteful campaign to keep the Marquis under lock and key in the 1770s and 1780s.

The potential symbolism of both violations (dildo, needle) in a personal authorial context has led to a number of critical interpretations of the entire scene based on anthropological and psychoanalytical theories.

Freudians have read the scene in terms of the male castration complex, so that through Eugénie, Sade enacts a deep-seated fantasy. Plaiting and weaving, to which sewing is closely related, are for Freud intrinsically feminine activities, associated symbolically with women's 'genital deficiency', so that as they weave, women symbolically reproduce the pubic hair with which nature hides what is not there. By strapping on the dildo and using it to rape her mother, Eugénie has already in a sense restored to herself the lost phallus. As she now sews up her mother's genitals, Eugénie might be said, on an unconscious level, to be 'covering up' its absence. Behind Eugénie, then, the male author is closing up the wound of castration, in order to assuage his castration fears.

The post-war French novelist Pierre Klossowski reads Sade generally in terms of what he calls a 'negative oedipal complex', according to which libidinal aggression turns itself against the mother in alliance with an all-powerful father. For Klossowski, the same scenario, of which the needle-scene is a perfect model, replays itself repeatedly throughout Sade's work: the father collaborates with the child to punish the mother and/or to destroy the family. We remember that, though physically absent, Eugénie's father has given full permission for the mother's chastisement. Dolmancé, in orchestrating the whole scene, can be said to deputize for the absent father.

These psychoanalytically-based approaches all place the author's unconscious fears and desires at the centre of his text, and seem to offer considerable insight into the relation between the two. Dolmancé's despair at the weakness that follows orgasm is a key motif in the Sadeian text, and similarly invites a psychoanalytical reading. The libertine must never allow himself any weakness, and if sex leaves him unavoidably weak, he is bound to hate the cause. This helps to explain the ambivalence towards women in Sade which we identified in the previous chapter: objects of desire on the one hand and contempt on the other, women make men hard but drain them post-coitally of strength.

This contempt for women is extended in the scene's closing lines to all those law-abiding members of society, for whom rape and torture are criminal acts. Only fools would call these crimes, Dolmancé implies, because nature allows them to occur. Since all events in nature must by definition be necessary to the preservation of balance and harmony, logically nothing in nature can be undesirable. Notions of what is right and wrong are, in any case, culturally and temporally relative, and to talk of some actions as good and others as bad is to ignore the reality of nature as amoral, devoid of all reason or sentiment, driven solely by the principle of self-interest.

The logical conclusion of this argument, if taken seriously, would, of course, lead to the gas-chambers of Dachau and the torture-cellars of the paedophile and child-murderer Dutroux. Yet, as is so often the case with Sade, we must beware of too literal a reading. Appearing in 1795 shortly after Sade's release from prison and only months after the fall of the despotic Robespierre, during a period of French history scarcely noted for its celebration of collective virtues and the brotherhood of man, *Philosophy in the Boudoir*'s vindication of individual tyranny and lust has a bitterly ironic ring.

10

SADE'S LEGACY

Fifth: Lastly, I absolutely forbid anyone to cut my body open on any pretext whatsoever. I ask most earnestly that it be kept in the chamber where I shall have died for forty-eight hours, then placed in a wooden coffin which shall not be nailed shut until the above-mentioned period of forty-eight hours has elapsed, whereupon the said coffin shall be nailed shut. During this interval, an express message shall be sent to Monsieur Le Normand, wood-merchant, of number one hundred and one, boulevard de l'Égalité, Versailles, asking him to come himself with a cart to fetch my body, and to transport it under his own escort in the said cart to the wood on my lands at Malmaison near Épernon in the commune of Émancé, where I wish it to be laid, without ceremony of any kind, in the first copse on the right as one enters this wood from the old château by the broad path dividing it. A ditch shall be dug in this copse by the tenant-farmer of Malmaison under the supervision of Monsieur Le Normand who shall not leave my body until after he has placed it in the said ditch. He may, if he wishes, be joined in this ceremony by those among my relatives or friends who, without pomp of any kind, shall have been good enough to show me this last mark of affection. Once the ditch has been covered over, it shall be strewn with acorns so that in time, as the earth upon the said ditch becomes green again and the copse grows back as dense as it was before, the traces of my grave may disappear from the face of the earth as I trust my memory shall fade from the minds of men, except, however, for that small number who have been kind enough to love me until the last and of whom I carry a sweet remembrance with me to the grave.

Done at Charenton-Saint-Maurice in sound mind and body this thirtieth day of January eighteen hundred and six.

Last Will and Testament, my translation

Sade's *Last Will and Testament* was written some eight years before his death. When the time finally came, his wishes were completely ignored by his surviving son, who arranged for the life-long atheist and scourge of all religions to be given a Christian burial in the small cemetery at the Charenton asylum where he had spent his last twelve years.

This well-known closing passage from the will is wholly consistent with Sade's atheistic philosophy and his theories of the eternal recycling of all matter. His fear of premature burial may have inspired Edgar Allan Poe, who had certainly read Sade. There is a touching concern that the ceremony be conducted as simply as possible: the transportation of his body in a cart like that of any peasant suggests a modesty that many might find surprising in the headstrong former aristocrat, and there is a moving hint that he would be pleased if those whom he loved and who loved him might attend. Above all, here, Sade is determined to ensure that, beyond the various modest bequests he has made earlier in the document (mostly to his companion, Madame Quesnet), his name does not live on. Sade therefore concludes what is intended to be a document detailing his legacy to the living by questioning the very notion of legacy. But how can Sade's inheritors forget if they have to remember to do so? And there is, of course, the small matter of Sade's writings, which he cannot have intended to perish with him. One would be forgiven, then, for thinking that there was a degree of disingenuousness in Sade's apparent aspiration to oblivion.

There is undoubtedly an element of self-dramatization in these lines. Sade the martyr of self-effacement hardly accords with the haughty, strong-willed personality we know from his correspondence. It is all very well to theorize about worms and regeneration in nature, as Sade does elsewhere (see Chapter 2), but the writer's own ego was too large to include himself in such a scenario. An intense desire to leave behind a legacy of writing that would explain his situation and vindicate him in the eyes of future readers is a primary motivation behind many of his writings, including the diaries he kept at Charenton in the 1800s. And if writing is a legacy, then reading must be in part about understanding what has been bequeathed. All of those who read Sade are therefore in this sense his inheritors, and as such we need to sort out exactly what it is that Sade has left us.[23]

In the realm of the medical and psychological sciences, Sade's *120 Days of Sodom*, in particular, prefigured and perhaps even inspired the taxonomic approach to human sexuality undertaken by Krafft-Ebing and Freud at the end of the nineteenth century (although Sade would certainly not have shared or approved of the normative attitudes favoured by sexologists and psychoanalysts – for Sade, there is no moral hierarchy of sexual activities, no concept of a division between the normal and the perverse).

Some have identified Sade's influence throughout twentieth-century popular culture, from mainstream examples to its seamier side. Angela Carter sees the innocent *Justine* and the vampish *Juliette* as two stereotypes of femininity that have helped to define the ingénues and seductresses of much Hollywood cinema, while the Marquis's dark shadow may also be seen hovering over any pornographic work of a sado-masochistic character (compare, for example, *Philosophy in the Boudoir* and certain sex-initiation scenes in the modern porn

movie). More generally, however, Sade has frequently been
hailed as a patron saint of the climate of sexual liberation and
permissiveness that changed attitudes and behaviour in the
West from the 1960s onwards, with its accompanying emphasis on hedonism and abandonment of conventional
religious values. It is scarcely legitimate, however, to make
such a connection. While Sade would certainly have approved
of these developments, the advent of the pill and a complexity of social factors were the real causes of a more permissive
society, not the reading of *Justine*. Moreover, the relaxation of
censorship laws that has occurred over the last forty years in
the West may have made Sade's writings more available, but
the demonization of both the man and his work is as ubiquitous as ever, even among the liberal middle classes. In 1992,
Nicolas Walter, a well-known anti-censorship campaigner
who actively defended Salman Rushdie and his publishers,
called Sade 'an evil writer'.[24]

Sadeian themes are equally identifiable in serious culture.
The surrealists' rediscovery of Sade at the beginning of the
last century – for the French poet Guillaume Apollinaire,
Sade was quite simply 'the freest spirit who ever lived' –
opened up the arts generally to an unfettered exploration of
sexual desire. For the leader of the surrealist movement in
France, André Breton, sadism is itself fundamentally surrealist: 'Sade is surrealist in his sadism,' he declares in *The
Surrealist Manifesto* of 1924. Sade's influence is clearly discernible, too, in twentieth-century trends towards extreme
art, from Surrealism, via Artaud's Theatre of Cruelty, to the
recent 'self-harm' experiments of some contemporary
British artists. Salvador Dalí, Georges Bataille and many
other modern writers, artists and film-makers have been
directly inspired by Sade's works. *The 120 Days of Sodom*, for
example, has provided themes and situations for films by

Luis Buñuel, Pier Paolo Pasolini and Peter Greenaway, among others.

Perhaps, though, Sade's most important bequest of all is less specific and more pervasive than any of these: the gift of a healthy scepticism at a time of multiplying fanaticisms, whether of a religious or a political kind. For Michel Foucault, Sade straddles the classical and the modern epochs. His work represents in its entirety a thorough going critique of the old monarchical and aristocratic world and of the religious belief that supported it, but also of the dangers of post-revolutionary despotism of any complexion, and this is a critique that went much further than that of any of his contemporaries. In this sense, Sade is one of the first powerful voices of a secular and ultimately more democratic modern world.

Sade's enduring legacy, then, is located less in the detail of his sexually violent scenarios or of his libertines' nihilistic and iconoclastic philosophies than in the central core of his thought, which shifted the emphasis away from a God-centred spirituality to a Man-centred materialism and which, in so doing, helped to sweep away the pernicious superstitions of the old theocratic order and contributed to the creation of a modern intellectual climate in which all absolutisms are regarded with suspicion. This legacy is wholly in keeping with the spirit of Sade's *Last Will and Testament*. The desire to disappear from the minds of all men relates, after all, to the man and not the work. The philosophical Sade, the Sade that endures, is to be found not in the biographical myths and historical uncertainties, but in the words that he wrote and the currents of thought that these words inspired.

NOTES

1 From this canon of writings, only a small number survived the storming of the Bastille in 1789. Sade had been imprisoned there until days before the ancient prison-fortress was invaded by the revolutionary mob, and was moved so suddenly to another prison that he had no time to assemble all of his manuscripts. The lost works included *The 120 Days of Sodom*, which did not surface again until the twentieth century.

2 *The Encyclopedia*, quoted by Gilbert Lély, *Sade* (Paris: Éditions Gallimard, 1967), p. 200.

3 See Jean Leduc, 'Les sources de l'athéisme et de l'immoralisme du marquis de Sade', *Studies on Voltaire and the Eighteenth Century* 68 (1969), 7–66, and Caroline Warman, *Sade: From Materialism to Pornography*, *Studies on Voltaire and the Eighteenth Century* 2002:01 (Oxford: Voltaire Foundation, 2002).

4 Lucille Margaret Kekewich, Introduction, Machiavelli, *The Prince* (Wordsworth Editions Ltd, 1997), xvi.

5 ibid.

6 ibid., Ch. 18: 'In What Manner Princes Should Keep Their Faith', p. 68.

7 See especially ibid., Ch. 19.

8 Lély, *Sade*, p. 159.

9 See Chapter 4 on politics: Sade composed one other '*Idée*', the 'Idea on the Method of Sanctioning of Laws'.

10 Angela Carter, *The Sadeian Woman. An Exercise in Cultural History* (London: Virago Press, 1979), pp. 91–2.

11 See Friedrich Nietzsche, *Human, All Too Human*. The nineteenth-century German philosopher certainly read Sade, and, as was observed in Chapter 1, his notion of the superman may well have been influenced by him.

12 The full sense of *jouissance* is hard to convey in English: semantically, it approximates to 'orgasm', but the French word somehow carries more cerebral connotations of pleasure extending as much to the mind as to the body.

13 For the modern French philosopher Michel Foucault, transgression is precisely about exceeding limits.

14 Bataille, *L'Érotisme* (Paris: Minuit, 1957), p. 65.

15 ibid., p. 295.

16 See Julia Kristeva, *Powers of Horror* (New York: Columbia University Press, 1982).

17 Geoffrey Bennington, 'Forget to Remember, Remember to Forget: Sade avec Kant', *Paragraph*, Vol. 23, No. 1, March 2000, pp. 75–86; this ref. p. 81.

18 ibid., p. 84.

19 The most accessible account of Bakhtin's theories is to be found in his essay 'Discourse in the Novel', in Michael Holquist (ed.), M. M. Bakhtin, *The Dialogic Imagination* (Austin: University of Texas Press, 1981).

20 Angela Carter, *The Sadeian Woman*, p. 27.

21 Angela Carter, speaking on *The Late Show*, BBC2, 1990.

22 Angela Carter, *The Sadeian Woman*, p. 135.

23 I am indebted to Geoffrey Bennington (op. cit.) for these observations on reading as a form of inheritance.

24 Nicolas Walter, 'Confront Sade, don't ban him', in *Index on Censorship* 1/1992, p. 7.

CHRONOLOGY

1740 2 June: birth of Donatien Alphonse François de Sade, lord of La Coste, Saumane and Mazan in Provence. He was brought up in the palace of the Prince de Condé, who was four years older.

1746 Sent to live with his uncle, the abbé de Sade, at Saumane in Provence.

1750 Pursues his studies at the Jesuit college of Louis-le-Grand in Paris. The Jesuits infect him with a life-long enthusiasm for the theatre.

1755 Appointed sub-lieutenant in the King's infantry regiment. In the course of active service in the Seven Years War is promoted to the rank of captain.

1763 17 May: marriage to Renée-Pélagie de Montreuil.
October: briefly imprisoned at Vincennes for allegedly whipping Jeanne Testard, a fan-maker.

1765 Liaison with Mademoiselle de Beauvoisin, an actress.

1767 Death of his father, the comte de Sade, and birth of his first son, Louis-Marie.

1768 The Rose Keller affair: imprisoned for six months initially at Saumur, then at Pierre-Encise near Lyons for alleged acts of libertinage, sacrilege and sadism on Easter Sunday in his house at Arcueil.

1769 Birth of his second son, Donatien-Claude-Armand.

1771 Birth of his daughter, Madeleine-Laure. Briefly imprisoned for debt.

1772 17 June: the Marseilles affair: Sade and his valet are found guilty of sodomy and attempted poisoning on the occasion of an orgy in Marseilles. Both flee to Italy, accompanied by Sade's young sister-in-law, Anne-Prospère. Sentenced to death *in absentia*, their effigies are burnt publicly at Aix.

8 December: arrested and imprisoned at Miolans in Piedmont.

1773 1 May: escapes and eventually returns to La Coste. Sade's mother-in-law, the Présidente de Montreuil, embittered by the seduction of Anne-Prospère, obtains a *lettre de cachet* for his arrest and imprisonment.

1775 Flees once again to Italy.

1777 Fresh scandals at La Coste, this time involving young girls employed at the château.

13 February: arriving in Paris too late to visit his mother before her death, Sade is arrested and imprisoned at Vincennes.

1778 The accusations of attempted poisoning having been dismissed, the death sentence imposed by the Aix parlement is lifted, but the Présidente uses her influence to obtain a new *lettre de cachet*. Sade escapes but is recaptured and returned to Vincennes. He will remain in prison now until the Revolution.

1781 Writes the first of a succession of plays, *The Inconstant*.

1782 Writes the *Dialogue Between a Priest and a Dying Man* and begins *The 120 Days of Sodom*.

1784 29 February: transferred from Vincennes to the Bastille.

1786 Writes the greater part of his 'philosophical' novel *Aline et Valcour*.

1787 Composition of *The Misfortunes of Virtue*, the first novella-length version of *Justine*. Begins writing his collection of short stories, originally entitled *Tales and Fabliaux of the Eighteenth Century by a Provençal Troubadour*, a selection of which will eventually be published in 1799 under the title *The Crimes of Love*.

1789 2 July: Sade incites the mob to riot from his cell window in the Bastille, telling them that prisoners are being murdered.

4 July: sent to the insane asylum at Charenton, leaving behind a number of manuscripts, including *The 120 Days of Sodom* which he will never see again.

14 July: the fall of the Bastille and the start of the Revolution.

1790 1 April: Sade is released following abolition of *lettres de cachet* by the new revolutionary government. Formal separation from Renée-Pélagie and start of a new relationship with Constance Quesnet, nicknamed 'Sensitive', which will last until his death. Actively involved in revolutionary politics, promoting hospital reform. Tries unsuccessfully to get his plays performed.

1791 Anonymous publication of *Justine, or the Misfortunes of Virtue*, the second version of the *Justine* narrative, and performance of his play *The Comte d'Oxtiern, or the Effects of Libertinism*.

1792 Composes various revolutionary essays, including *The Idea on the Method for the Sanctioning of Laws*.

1793 Publishes a pamphlet in honour of Marat following his murder by Charlotte Corday. When the opportunity presents itself, Sade, who has been appointed a judge in his revolutionary section, does not sentence his in-laws to death. Suspected of moderation and royalist sympathies, Sade is arrested in December.

1794 Sade escapes death owing to a bureaucratic error, and is eventually released at the end of the Terror, following the fall and execution of Robespierre.

1795 Penniless owing to the loss of his lands and property in the Revolution, Sade tries to stage more plays. Publishes *Aline and Valcour*, and, anonymously, *Philosophy in the Boudoir*.

1799 Anonymous publication of *The New Justine, or the Misfortunes of Virtue, followed by the History of Juliette, her Sister, or the Prosperities of Vice*, and publication in Sade's own name of *The Crimes of Love*. Works as a prompt in a Versailles theatre for 40 sous a day.

1801 Sade arrested at his publishers in April for authorship of 'obscene' writings, and imprisoned at Sainte-Pélagie.

1803 Transferred to Bicêtre, then to Charenton.

1804 Sade's continued detention justified by the invention of a new medical condition, 'libertine dementia'.

1807 Confiscation of the libertine novel *The Days at Florbelle, or Nature unveiled*, begun in 1804. The manuscript will be destroyed at the behest of his younger son after his death.

1808 Organizes theatrical performances, using asylum inmates and professional actresses.

1812–13 Writes *Adelaide of Brunswick, Princess of Saxony*, *The Secret History of Isabelle of Bavaria* and *The Marquise de Gange*, all conventional historical novels.

1813–14 Affair with the sixteen-year-old laundry-maid Madeleine Leclerc.

1814 2 December: Sade's death, followed by interment in the Charenton cemetery with full religious rites.

SUGGESTIONS FOR FURTHER READING

1. Primary Texts

The newcomer to Sade, who may wish to begin with the least cruel of the 'libertine' works, is advised to read them in the following order: *Philosophy in the Boudoir, Justine, The New Justine, Juliette, The 120 Days of Sodom*. The rest of Sade's *œuvre* may be read in any order, according to individual taste. Most of Sade's works have been translated into English except for *Aline et Valcour*. *La Nouvelle Justine* has been translated but is not currently in print. The most widely available editions of other works are listed below:

Juliette, translated by Austryn Wainhouse (London: Arrow Books Ltd, 1991; translation, 1968).

Marquis de Sade, Justine, Philosophy in the Bedroom, and Other Writings, compiled and translated by Richard Seaver and Austryn Wainhouse (New York: Grove Weidenfeld, 1990). The volume includes the second *Justine*, *Dialogue between a Priest and a Dying Man* and *Last Will and Testament*.

Marquis de Sade: Letters from Prison, translated by Richard Seaver (London: Harvill Press, 2000).

The Crimes of Love, translated by Margaret Crosland (Dufour Editions, 1996).

The Misfortunes of Virtue and Other Early Tales, translated by David Coward (Oxford: Oxford University Press, 1999).

The Mystified Magistrate and Other Tales (Arcade Books, 2001).

The 120 Days of Sodom and Other Writings, compiled and translated by Austryn Wainhouse and Richard Seaver (London: Arrow Books, 1990).

A slightly abridged version of 'Note on the Novel' may be found in *Yale French Studies* No. 35 (1965).

All translations are from the above editions unless otherwise stated.

2. Biographies

Bongie, L. L., *Sade: A Biographical Essay* (Chicago & London: The University of Chicago Press, 1998).

Gorer, G., *The Life and Ideas of the Marquis de Sade* (New York: W. W. Norton, 1963; first published in London in 1934).

Lever, M., *Donatien Alphonse François, Marquis de Sade* (Paris: Librairie Arthème Fayard, 1991); English translation: Lever, M., *Marquis de Sade: A Biography*, translated by A. Goldhammer (London: HarperCollins, 1993).

du Plessix Gray, F., *At Home with the Marquis de Sade* (New York: Penguin Books, 1999).

Schaeffer, N., *The Marquis de Sade: A Life* (London: Hamish Hamilton Ltd, 1999).

Thomas, D., *The Marquis de Sade* (London: Allison & Busby, 1992).

3. Further Reading in English

NB: This section includes English translations of some works originally published in French.

Airaksinen, T., *The Philosophy of the Marquis de Sade* (London & New York: Routledge, 1995). This densely written study might prove daunting for some readers, but it does have the virtue, exceptionally in Sade criticism, of focusing solely on the philosophical thought.

Allison, D. B., Roberts, M. S., and Weiss, A. S. (eds.), *Sade and the Narrative of Transgression* (Cambridge: Cambridge University Press, 1995). This volume brings together in English fourteen essays by some of the best-known Sade scholars of the last thirty years.

Barthes, R., *Sade, Fourier, Loyola* (Johns Hopkins University Press, 1997). A brilliantly original approach, full of aphoristic gems, and highly readable.

Bataille, Georges, *Eroticism: Death and Sensuality* (City Lights Books, 1991). Chapters 5 and 6 are devoted to Sade. Difficult territory without a guide.

Beauvoir, Simone de, 'Must We Burn Sade?', translated by Annette Michelson (London and New York: Nevill, 1953); also in *The 120 Days of Sodom and Other Writings*, edited and translated by Austryn Wainhouse and Richard Seaver (New York: Grove Press; London: Arrow, 1990). The well-known French feminist's lengthy and lucid essay on Sade draws heavily on existentialist and psychoanalytic theory.

Carter, A., *The Sadeian Woman* (London: Virago Press, 1979). An intelligent and inspired analysis of the feminine in Sade.

Dworkin, A., *Pornography: Men Possessing Women* (London: Women's Press, 1981). Chapter 3 is infuriatingly one-sided, demonizing Sade as the quintessential woman-hating pornographer. Worth reading as one of the more intelligent examples of anti-Sade rhetoric, although Dworkin shows absolutely no sensitivity to the literary dimensions of the works.

Frappier-Mazur, L., *Writing the Orgy: Power and Parody in Sade* (Philadelphia: University of Pennsylvania Press, 1996). A psychoanalytically informed study which focuses on *Juliette*. Makes a persuasive case for reading Sade's fictions as an anal-phallic universe.

Hénaff, Marcel, *Sade: The Invention of the Libertine Body* (University of Minnesota Press, 1999). Heavy-going but brilliant and original.

Klossowski, P., *Sade My Neighbour* (London: Quartet Books, 1992). The first to suggest, in 1947, that Sade's atheism is actually a case of Freudian denial, that to rail against God with such vehemence and frequency is in fact to acknowledge his existence. Difficult but rewarding.

Le Brun, A., *Sade: A Sudden Abyss* (City Lights Books, 1991). The *grande dame* of Sade studies, the author sets out a vigorously argued and well-researched case for viewing Sade as the first philosopher of the body in the modern era. Le Brun is the editor of the Complete Works published in the 1980s by J.-J. Pauvert.

Paglia, C., *Sexual Personae. Art and Decadence from Nefertiti to Emily Dickinson* (New York: Vintage Books, 1991). Various passages on Sade are characteristically quirky, forthright, brilliant. Paglia's Sade is a realist who paints nature not in the rose-tinted perspective of a Rousseau but as she truly is, 'pagan cannibal, her dragon jaws spitting sperm and spittle'.

Paulhan, J., 'The Marquis de Sade and His Accomplice', in *Marquis de Sade, Justine, Philosophy in the Bedroom, and Other Writings* (New York: Grove Weidenfeld, 1990), pp. 3–36. Argues the case that there is a psychological and emotional attachment on the author's part to Justine.

Phillips, John, *Sade: The Libertine Novels* (London: Pluto Press, 2001). A detailed introductory study to the four libertine novels, aimed at the student and the interested general reader.

Shattuck, R., *Forbidden Knowledge: From Prometheus to Pornography* (New York: St Martin's Press, 1996). Chapter VII seeks to establish the pernicious influence of Sade's works on human behaviour. In the book's opening pages, the author warns teachers and parents that the chapter does not make appropriate reading for children and minors.

4. Filmography

This list is restricted to films which, regardless of quality, have been directly based on Sade's life or work. Those originally made in English are asterisked.

L'Âge d'or (Luis Buñuel and Salvador Dalí, 1930)
Le Vice et la Vertu (Roger Vadim, 1963)
La Voie lactée (Luis Buñuel, 1969)
*De Sade (Cyril Enfield, 1971)
*Peter Weiss's *Marat-Sade* (Peter Brook, 1973)
Salo (Pier Paolo Pasolini, 1975)
Marquis (Roland Topor and Henri Xhonneux, 1988)
*Quills (Philip Kaufman, 2000)
Sade (Benoît Jacquot, 2000)

INDEX